Someone
Special
starring
YOUth

Someone Special
starring YOUth

George D. Durrant

Bookcraft
Salt Lake City, Utah

Library of Congress Catalog Card Number: 76-45722
ISBN 0-88494-311-9

9 10   89 88 87 86 85 84

Contents

Preface

The message of this book is for you—the youth of the Church.

The inward search for oneself and one's place in life is most intense during the teenage years. One often feels considerable inward emotional pain as he or she traverses the shifting plains that separate childhood from adulthood. Some feel that during these years they are sort of halfway to nowhere.

But deep within each of us a star shines. It is the light that, when it finally breaks through the fog and haze of self-doubt, causes each of us to know that he or she is a child of God and is special.

Recorded on these pages are some of my memories of those difficult years in my own life. And from these memories, and with the perspective of time, I have prayerfully tried in this book to expose principles that will help others who now feel as I once felt.

Each of us was sent to earth to be a "star"—to be someone special. Some never really come to fully believe that. Thus their light remains hidden by the mists and clouds of inferior feelings and the lack of faith in themselves and in God.

But there is a special place for each of us in our

Preface

Heavenly Father's plan. We are not in competition with anyone else but only with ourselves. When we come to know that we are special, that does not disqualify anyone else from the same distinction. For all of the sons and daughters of God are special.

Three of my children were swinging in a park. Two of them had learned to pump themselves in swings. Our little daughter had not yet mastered this skill. The two who could pump themselves were on the two outside swings and the little girl, who was only moving because of a breeze, was in the middle one.

Devin, on one outside swing, was going as high as the swing would allow. He noticed that Kathryn, on the other outside swing, was doing the same. He shouted, "I'm keeping up with Kathryn." Swinging in unison with him, Kathryn shouted back, "I'm keeping up with Devin." Little Marinda, who was scarcely moving, looked first at one and then the other and then humbly said, "I'm just keeping up with myself."

That is the race you are to run, a race in which your eternal goal is to keep up with that spark of divinity which is best described as *yourself*.

Perhaps reading and considering this book will help you to believe that you in reality are "someone special." And as you strive to keep up with that belief, you will truly be a "star."

Chapter 1
Me Special?

The group had just finished playing a recent hit and were bunched together discussing what their next number would be. I approached the young man who played the guitar and who was the leader of the three musicians. "It's late," I said. "We'd better stop now and let the kids go home."

To my surprise my words angered him, and he snapped back, "We aren't ready to quit yet."

I replied with haste. "The dance is over, there's school tomorrow and these kids have got to get home."

He responded, "We are going to play another song." At that he started to play and his friends joined in. I was no longer able to hear or be heard, so I silently and reluctantly agreed that they were indeed going to play another number.

I positioned myself near the electrical outlets and waited while they finished what seemed to me to be an unusually long song. At the appropriate time I pulled out their power cords and announced, "That's all for tonight."

This act on my part greatly irritated the young leader. As I walked a few steps towards him, he glared at me and said, "You old guys are always trying to run things and tell everybody what to do."

I tried to remain calm as I replied: "Can't you understand? It's late. We've had a good time and we appreciate your coming to play for us. But now it's time to quit and go home."

His eyes seemed filled with hate as he announced, "This is the last time I'll ever play for a dance in this church."

By this time some of the youth from the ward had gathered around to see what the problem was. I tried to reason with the young man, but my every word seemed to add fuel to his anger. His attack shifted from me to the Church. He made several negative remarks about religion. By now he realized that he had an audience of young people, and this seemed to give him a desire to show the Church up in front of them.

He asked me a question which he felt put the Church in a bad light. I did my best to answer. He then asked another question. Now we had a real discussion going on religion, and many of the youth were listening. As we talked, he slowly turned from his anger and became almost pleasant.

It was getting even later than it had been before. I advised him that we'd better get home or we'd all be in trouble. He smiled and agreed. "But before we part," I said, "I'd like you to give me your name and address."

This request seemed to ruffle him a little and he asked, "What for?"

I replied, "I just want to keep in touch with you."

"Why?" he asked, almost suspiciously.

"I don't know," I replied. "I guess it's because I feel that you're a special kind of guy."

2

"Special!" he laughed. "Me special! That's a joke. I'm about as special as nothing. What do you mean, anyway?"

"I mean . . . well, there's just something about the way you play music, the way you smile, the way you talk, and just sort of the way you are. It all goes together and makes you a special guy."

He looked into my eyes as if to silently ask, "Do you really mean that?" I believe he detected that I was completely sincere. His whole soul seemed subdued. His eyes moistened with tears.

I wondered at the time why my words had such an impact upon him. It wasn't until some time later that I learned that I was the only person he could recall who had ever told him that he was special.

Finally he asked, "Have you got a pen?" He wrote the name Mike and then added his last name and his address.

The next day I couldn't get him off my mind. I wrote him a letter in which I repeated that I felt that he was a special person. I went on to express my appreciation for his group coming and playing at our dance.

Days, weeks, and even months went by and I didn't see or hear from Mike. Then one day I received a letter from him. As I opened the envelope, my mind focused back to the night when we'd met for the one and only time. His letter read:

"Dear Brother Durrant:

"I received your letter some months ago. I read it and put it in my drawer. Yesterday I was cleaning up my room

3

getting ready to spend six weeks in jail. I saw your letter and I read it again. You said that you felt I was special. You said that at the dance too. Why do you feel that way when I've had so much trouble?

"How could you believe something like that about someone like me?

"I wish I could believe that there was anything at all special about me.

"Nobody but you ever said I was special. Do you really believe I am? If you do, please come to the jail and see me.

"Please come and help me. I kind of feel like maybe somehow I am special. At least I'd like to be, but I don't even know how. Please help me.

"Love,

"Mike—your special friend."

Let's leave Mike for a little while. After all, he's in jail, so he won't be going anywhere. Perhaps we are all sort of in a jail too. And the key to our getting out and really being free is to come to know that we, each of us, are special.

I feel that I'm special. How about you? Do you feel that you are? It's not always an easy feeling to get. And sometimes there seems to be a good amount of evidence to prove that we are not special.

I've found that it is easier to feel special at age forty than it was to feel that way at age fourteen and fifteen. My main qualification for writing this book is that I have a vivid memory of my junior and senior high school days. I recall the frustrations and insecurities I felt. I could believe

4

many things back then. But the one thing that I could hardly believe at all was that I was then, or ever would be, "special."

I shall rely upon the memory of my youth as I explore with you the possibility of helping you become aware that you are someone special.

My early years were not exactly like yours. We all grew up under different circumstances. But my feelings are much the same as yours. We would all like to be someone special—someone who is really a somebody; someone who is admired in some way; someone who has friends; someone who is needed and wanted; someone who can do something better than almost anyone else.

As I grew up, my mother treated me as if I was special. I was the youngest of nine children and was thus her baby. Some people said that she "spoiled" me. They would say to her, "You are spoiling him by doing so much for him and by treating him so well." I'd think: "Why don't you mind your own business? I don't mind being spoiled."

But at school it was different. There I quickly learned that I wasn't really that special. I recall that one day when I was in the second grade the teacher showed us a beautiful book titled *Snow White*. (Snow White was new then.) She said she had two such books and that she was going to give one to the boy and one to the girl who proved by their work that they were the best students in the class for one month. I wanted one of those books with all my heart. As the days passed I tried to be the best. On the day she was to award the books I sat excitedly in my seat. I was certain that I would be a winner. But I wasn't. I'll always remember her giving the book to my friend. In my mind I decided at that

5

time that maybe he was a little more special than I was. That was a sad day for me.

As I progressed through school I received more and more evidence that convinced me that in comparison with many of my classmates I really wasn't very special. Spelling and other subjects were difficult for me. But there was one bright spot, and that was sports. I felt that I was special in physical activities. Then one day at a school picnic we had a foot race in the park. I desperately wanted to win. But I didn't. Three or four other boys beat me. After that I didn't know what there was at all that made me special.

All throughout my school days, when I'd arrive home from school my mother would make me a peanut butter sandwich. Sometimes my brothers and sisters would say, "Let him make his own sandwich." But she would say: "Never mind. I like to do it for him." Then when just Mother and I were alone, I'd say, "The reason that I like you to make sandwiches for me is that when you make them they taste better." And she'd say, "I like to do it for you, George, because I love you and because you are special."

As I arrived in junior high school I came to know many feelings of insecurity. And in senior high those feelings had increased. In my younger years my mother would hold me on her lap and I'd feel better. But now that I was in high school I felt a little embarrassed about sitting on her lap. For that reason I wouldn't do so until I had pulled the drapes so that no one could look in. She would run her fingers through my hair and she'd say, "George, you are special." That would make me feel so good; because I felt deep down in my heart that she was right.

6

But at the same time I wondered why no one else seemed to know that I was special. I wondered why the girls didn't know. I was never overburdened with invitations to Girls' Day dances and things like that. I wondered why my classmates didn't know I was special and elect me to at least a minor student body office. I wondered why the teachers didn't know and give me better grades. And I wondered why the basketball coach didn't know and put me in the game before the very end.

But most of all I wondered why I knew I was special, yet on the other hand I couldn't really seem to act and feel special. I wondered why I couldn't have more confidence; why I couldn't have a better personality; why I couldn't do things better. I felt deep down in my mind that I really did have something to offer but I didn't know how to let it loose. I felt just as much in jail as my friend Mike.

For that reason I write to you, my young friends. Especially to you who feel as I felt. I write to try to soothe the pain that you sometimes feel. I write in the hope that my words will help you to know how to make it through. Perhaps no one else has ever told you what I am about to tell you, but please believe me when I say "You are special." If you'll believe that, although you might hurt at times, you'll make it. And someday you'll know just how special you really are.

One day my four-year-old son was hiding from me. I knew where he was, because I could see his feet sticking out from behind a chair. But wishing to contribute to his fun, I shouted, "Where is he?" Then I added, "I think he is in the bookcase." I removed several books and announced, "He isn't there." Then I said, "I think he is in the lamp." I turned it off and on and exclaimed, "He isn't

7

there.'' Then I went near his hiding-place and stated in a loud voice: ''I can't find him. I guess I'll have to go and buy an ice cream cone all by myself.'' At that point he jumped from behind the chair and announced, ''Daddy, I've found myself.''

Within each of us is a divine star which is his true self. But often that special star is hidden by an overcast sky. The real self can't seem to shine through. Our life's purpose is to push aside the clouds and find that real self. But to find oneself is quite a task. Others can help but the struggle is basically the individual's alone. It's a quest that is sometimes painful, but that is all right. Struggling with the pain makes us grow, and when we do shine we do so all the brighter.

A man was wrestling on the floor with his two little sons. He grew tired before they did, which is often the case when fathers and sons wrestle. To get some rest, he decided to act as though he had fallen asleep. As he lay there the boys wondered if he had died. The older of the two, not knowing what else to do, reached down and with his thumb pulled open one of his father's eyelids. Then he looked at the smaller boy and reassuringly announced, ''He's still in there!''

You are in there, my young friends. The divine star that is really you is glowing deep within your soul. And you are special. Now is the time to begin to truly find your special self. If you desire, with the help of God you will in time emerge on the horizon as a bright and special star.

And when you do, you will have fulfilled the purpose for which you came down from heaven to dwell in an earth that needs special people to be a light for all to follow. And someday you'll be able to stand before God, and with perfect joy say, ''Father, I found myself.''

8

Chapter 2
The Common Ailment— an Inferiority Complex

I have not always been the tall handsome fellow that I am now. (I feel free to describe myself as "handsome" in this book of many words and no pictures.)

I didn't feel as though I was very handsome in junior and senior high school.

Not only that, but I didn't feel I was as big as I should be, as smart as I wanted to be, as popular as I longed to be, or as athletic as everyone seemed to feel I ought to be. And all of these feelings together added up to a grand total which was equal to an inferiority complex.

Not wishing to brag, I humbly submit that I feel that my inferiority complex was far superior to yours. In this chapter I shall state my reasons for feeling like an inferior teenager, and then when you and I meet you can present your case. I'm sure that you will have a case to present, because it is amazing how almost all of us have at one time or another been afflicted by this great epidemic of self-doubt and insecurity which we call an inferiority complex.

To joke about personal feelings of inferiority is much easier at age forty than it was at age fourteen. As a teenager, such feelings often made me want to cry but never did they make me want to laugh.

It was not easy, as many of you will know, for me to be small of stature when I wanted to be large. As a sixth grader I was just about the biggest boy in the class. In the seventh grade I didn't grow and some of the boys passed me by in size. The eighth grade was also a static growth year for me and then I was but the size of the average. I again failed to grow in the ninth grade. I recall that in that year we lined up in a P. E. class according to size. I was one of the smallest of the group.

Oh, how that worried me! I wanted to be big. I felt that in order to be special I had to be big. My brother just three years older than me was a virtual giant. I prayed that I'd grow. I ate Wheaties and other foods that radio announcers told me would make me grow. I'd stand and stretch. I tried everything I could think of, but I couldn't grow. And I began to think, "I shall forever be a small, immature boy while all of the other boys are growing and becoming men." I didn't know then that the passing of time was a friend who would eventually help me out.

People who knew my family to be large of stature would ask me, "When are you going to grow?" I'd feel like saying, "I don't know, but when I do I shall send you a postcard."

My dream was to be a great basketball player. My brother was all-state at the time. I had the desire to be as good as he was, but I didn't seem to have the ability nor the size. I was often asked, "Are you going to be as good as your brother?" I could tell that the person asking didn't think that I would be. I'd reply that I didn't know. But oh, how I wanted to be! I'd spend endless hours out by the barn shooting at the makeshift goal that I had fashioned from a barrel top. Such practice was all right on cold days when the barnyard floor was frozen. But as spring came

10

on, things got a bit sloppy. Even that didn't stop me. I've never been much of a dribbler, however.

As my high school years came on, my almost endless hours of practicing didn't quite do the job. It became apparent to me that, though I was better at the game than some, there were many who were better than I. And all of my wishes couldn't change that.

I made the team all right, but all that earned me was the right to a front row seat. Now as I look back I realize that the coach must have thought I was special because he wanted me to sit with him all during the game, or at least until the score was 63 to 22 in our favor. At that point someone would shout, "Put George in." Getting in the game so near the end caused me to feel even more inferior.

Being a reserve on a ball team is really nothing to be ashamed of. But I had had such high hopes and a family reputation to uphold. Besides that I had put all my eggs in that basket, and when I failed in that one thing I concluded in my mind that I had failed in everything. Others can sit on the bench and feel good, but they are those who find fulfillment in other directions.

I didn't tell anyone how I felt. Such matters at that time seemed far too personal, and I supposed that talking about them might even enhance the pain. I wish now that I could have told my dad, or a teacher, or my bishop. I know now that just talking about it would have helped.

These feelings of not measuring up carried over into almost all other facets of my life. I remember the talk that I prepared for the time of my nomination as student body president. But I never gave it because I was never nominated as student body president. No one knew I wanted to run for president because I was afraid to

12

mention it. I feared that if I ran I'd lose. My delicate ego couldn't have stood that.

I also wanted to be popular with the girls. I wanted to stand in the halls and talk to them and make them laugh. I wanted them to think that I was a neat guy. But I was bashful and shy and had a feeling that they couldn't possibly be interested in me.

I'll rest my case at this point, because I feel that you can see that I really did have a superior inferiority complex. But then you probably do too—at least, many of you do. You've got your own reasons for feeling inferior. Even you athletes and you student body leaders and you cheerleaders and you marching girls and you beauty queens have struggles with self-doubts and personal insecurities.

I recall a youth conference at which the young people were having a testimony meeting. From the back of the hall came a most beautiful girl. Her bishop, who was sitting by me, quietly said, "She won the teenage beauty pageant for the state and was a runner-up in the national contest, where she was also chosen as Miss Congeniality."

As part of her warm and inspiring words, this beautiful girl said, amidst her tears: "My dear friends, I love you. You all have so much to offer and I have so little. For years I have felt that I didn't measure up. I have had feelings that I had no worth as a person; I've felt so inferior to all of you. But you've loved me and accepted me until now I'm coming to accept myself."

When she concluded her remarks, almost all of us were filled with a deep joy. We all felt that she, like us, was a struggler. She had so much to recommend her in the way of outward beauty, yet there she was within her soul,

13

searching for and longing to attain those inward feelings that would enable her to say, "I am special." Yes, inferiority feelings are common to almost all of us. And just knowing that others also struggle is a bit of a step toward feeling special.

In the first chapter I told you about Mike. I went to the jail to see him. The guards took me to a small room where I awaited his arrival. Finally a door opened and he entered. I arose and we shook hands. I held on until he looked me in the eyes. We sat down and talked. Finally we discussed what he should do after he would be released from jail. He said, "I've never told anyone this before, but what I'd really like to do is study to become a lawyer."

He'd explained earlier about his court case. At that time I'd been impressed with his ability to express himself. And it had occurred to me then that he sounded like a lawyer. I told him that now and he seemed pleased. I encouraged him and told him that he ought to set a goal to enter college and to strive to become a lawyer.

He looked away from me as he said, "I could never make it."

I asked, "Why not?"

He replied, "I could never be a lawyer. I could never be anything that took any brains."

"Sure you can," I said.

"I can't," he said emphatically. "All my life I've been a failure. I've never been able to do anything right. I'm stupid. I'm no good."

We changed the subject. As we talked, I was impressed with his warm smile. He told me he could play

14

five musical instruments and that his favorite pursuit was composing and playing his own music on the piano. I was amazed at his use of words, which told me that he was a man of unusual intellectual ability. It was hard to believe that such a man as he could describe himself so inaccurately. He had the common ailment (an inferiority complex) and he had an almost fatal case.

Mike, myself, and you—all of us have feelings about ourselves. And when all the surface froth has been blown away, many of us feel inferior. But is this so bad? The only real tragedy is what we sometimes do about these feelings.

To deal with personal insecurities we need first to realize that we are not alone in such struggles. At high school dances I felt that everyone there was watching me to see if I was putting my feet in the right places. Now I know that their main concern wasn't for me but for themselves. They were more concerned with what was wrong with themselves than they were about what was wrong with me. Someone once said to me, "George, you wouldn't worry what people think about you if you knew how seldom they do." That's both a comforting and a "discomforting" thought. But for our purposes it helps us to know that people don't spend all their time looking at us to try to discover our self-supposed weaknesses. Thus the only real observer of your problems is yourself.

To know one's weaknesses can be a blessing. The Lord tells us in the Book of Mormon that if we will pray to him he will show us our weaknesses. He wants us to be aware of our weaknesses. He promises us that if we will humble ourselves and have faith in him he will help us and our weaknesses will become our strengths.

15

If, for example, you feel that your mind isn't able to grasp certain school work, and if you feel that that is a weakness, it could cause you to try harder and thus develop qualities of ambition that will make you strong. If you feel that your nose is too long, you will be apt to try to make people forget that by having a positive personality that will make people love you in spite of your imperfect face. If you feel yourself too tall, you can stand up straight and your height will make you majestic.

And above all else, your feelings of inferiority can cause you to develop a special feeling of love for all others who you suppose might also suffer in the same painful way. And as that happens, you will be able to develop the greatest gift of all, the gift of charity or pure love.

On the other hand, if feelings of inferiority act as road blocks, then and only then do you have a real problem. If, because speaking in front of people frightens you, you refuse to speak, then you are in trouble. The fear isn't the trouble. Almost all of us have that. The refusal to ''do'' in spite of fear is the problem. The refusal to try out for the team, the club, the election, the part in the play, all because you fear that you might fail—that is the problem.

A friend of mine wished me well as I departed on my mission. I asked if he'd soon follow. His response was: ''Oh, no! I wouldn't dare knock on doors and try to teach people. It would scare me to death!'' I thought: ''What does that have to do with it? It scares me to go too, but I'm going.'' And I did and he didn't. And what a difference it has made!

So if you've been caught up by the disease of feeling inferior because your face is too round, or your figure is not perfect, or you're too short, or you're too tall, or your hair won't seem to comb the way you want it to, or you don't seem to come from the most wealthy family, or you aren't able to play ball, or you didn't quite get in the drill team, or you don't feel that you've got as much personality as you want, or you don't seem to be able to do as well in school as others—then what? Remember, if it isn't one thing you feel inferior about, you'll find something else, because that's the nature of almost all of us. These are the frustrations that come to you, but you can fight your way through them because, remember, "You are special." Special people feel inferior at times and they hurt at times. But they still keep moving toward their destiny as a child of God. Feelings of inferiority can eventually become the foundation for strength and compassion. Special people are often those shaped by the hurt and struggles of life.

Feelings of inferiority are a thick cloud cover over the star that shines deep within your soul. You must not let these dark feelings forever hide your special self. Be friendly, try out for the team, take part in school activities. Go forward in spite of your fears and doubts.

The chapters which follow offer suggestions on how the clouds can be pushed aside. As that happens, your former insecurities will have made you strong. And your special star will be brighter than words can ever say.

Chapter 3
Dream of Being Special

I've never been too good as a night dreamer but as a daydreamer I feel like a champion. I've even daydreamed of owning a 1949 Studebaker, and I'll bet you've never done that. It happened this way.

As I have said, I wasn't exactly the most preferred of all the young men at my high school. In my mind I came to the conclusion that one of the things that was holding me back socially was the fact that I didn't own a car. I supposed that if I had a car, that would solve a multitude of problems and would be the solution to all my feelings of inferiority. But to own a car appeared to be an impossibility, so I didn't even daydream about it. I've never believed in dreaming about impossibilities. I deal strictly in possibilities; I go as far as remote possibilities, but no further.

But suddenly a brand new car became a possibility, and thus my dream of a 1949 Studebaker was born.

In the spring of my junior year in high school I learned that many farmers had made thousands of dollars by growing celery during the previous summer. I knew a farmer who would provide the land and all the financing for any crop I wanted to plant, care for, and harvest. He and I would then share the profits. I decided that celery

was the crop and that my half of the profits would be one fancy Studebaker.

The beginning of the summer found me bent over in a large field planting little celery plants. In my dream they weren't celery plants at all, but instead each one was a little part of my new car.

All summer I labored in that field. As the sun bore down I didn't mind the heat because of my dream. As I went up and down the rows with my hoe cutting the weeds and loosening the soil, I wasn't in the field at all; instead I was dream-driving my fine car. As the sweat dropped from my forehead I'd see (in my mind) myself arriving at school and parking the car. Girls would be standing nearby smiling and hinting that they would like to go for a ride with me after school. As the summer wore on, the celery grew and my dream looked more and more probable.

One thing you should know about 1949 Studebakers is that the front and back looked almost identical. I really liked that feature. In my dreams in the celery field I'd drive my car down the road and one of my classmates would say, "There goes old George." And another would say, "How do you know he is going. He might be coming—you can't tell with a Studebaker."

Just as my crop was ready for harvest, the market became flooded with celery. The price dropped drastically and my dream crumbled into the celery-laden soil. With my meager profits I had to settle for a bicycle instead of a Studebaker.

I don't consider this a sad story. To me it was a happy one. I'm glad I had that dream. It didn't come true, but it surely made my summer pleasant. Dreams don't all have to come true to be worthwhile. Dreams have value

20

because they are something that can get inside of our minds. And once inside they can chase away all sorts of miserable, negative, hopeless ideas. Such unhappy ideas come as uninvited guests and can only be evicted by the power of possible, positive dreams.

For example, many is the night that I sat on the bench and watched a game in which I'd longed to play. As I trudged home through the snow, I'd pass the stream at the bottom of the hill, then I'd turn left through the windy and wooded Old Mill Lane. I'd pass the flour mill, cross over the creek, and turn up the alpine road and finally arrive home. As I walked along alone I'd hurt inside and feel that life just wasn't fair. But then into the back of my mind a little dream would creep in and begin to push out the painful inferior feelings. Soon the dream would have center stage of my mind, and I'd project myself forward to Monday. Monday in practice, I'd do well; Tuesday I'd be superb; Wednesday in scrimmage I'd really come through; and Friday I'd get in the game and I'd help the team win. Now I felt better. My dream, a possible dream, had driven remorse from my mind and had made things seem all right.

I suppose my talent for dreaming began when I was a young child. With all my brothers and sisters away at school and with no friends nearby, I grew lonely. To solve that problem I created an imaginary friend. I gave him the name Purnham Purnham. (Strange that that name I invented so long ago was so much like my wife's, Marilyn Burnham.) Purnham Purnham was a good friend. When I'd play games I shot a marble for me and then one for him. If he began to win, I'd get angry and just dissolve him. I've always reserved the right to dissolve or, better still, to revise my dreams.

Long after Purnham Purnham was last dissolved, my talent for dreaming continued to save me from despair.

My desire to be popular with the girls and my inability to do that caused me real frustration. But my "possible" dreams came to my rescue. As a sophomore I saw a junior going down the hall of the school with his arm around a girl. I dreamed that when I became a junior I'd do that. And that made me feel all right about not doing it as a sophomore. When I was a junior I saw a senior going down the hall with his arm around a girl. Again I dreamed that I'd do that as a senior. And again I felt that I was all right. As a senior I dreamed I'd do that in college. In college I dreamed that I'd do it after my mission. And after my mission—well, then I did it. And the girl became my wife. My dream gave me considerable mileage before it became a reality.

Before leaving the subject of popularity with those of the opposite sex, I want to mention my high school sweetheart. Actually she never knew she was my sweetheart because I never told her. I wouldn't have dared do that. I liked her too much to risk telling her. But I daydreamed about her often. She was a special sort of a girl and her name was Louise. I used to look at a map of the Southern states. My name is George and so I'd look at Georgia. Then I'd look at Louisiana and see them both in the same area. I'd get so excited that I just couldn't study geography.

I know a girl now who has a dream boyfriend. I'm glad she has, because it brings her happiness. He doesn't know how she feels, but that doesn't matter. It helps her when the real live dates are few and far between. I hope you have a dream boy or dream girl. In high school such a dream sweetheart is almost better than the real thing.

22

So to you girls who don't get a lot of dates, or who perhaps get none at all, I suppose it's all right to worry about it and to even cry about it. But while you are doing that, pick out a really fine fellow and dream about him. That will do much to soothe the worry and to dry up the tears.

Sometimes things get us down and we think all roads ahead are blocked. That's what my friend Mike felt. I asked him about his dreams and he said he didn't have any. He said he just wanted to see what he could do tomorrow but he didn't know where he wanted to go and didn't know what he wanted to be. I have told you about his desire to be a lawyer, but a dream is no good unless you're willing to go after it. You can't say you've got a dream and then say, "But I know I can never achieve that dream." There's no good in having a dream like that. Good dreams often come true, but seldom do they do so without effort.

In our many dreams there ought to be some in which we dream about something just down the road—something that is going to happen to us soon. If it doesn't happen we shouldn't be heartbroken, except maybe for a little while. We can then pick up the pieces and say: "I will revise my dreams. There are some things out there for me to reach."

When I got out of high school and into college I found out I wasn't going to realize my dream of being a big college basketball player, so I dreamed of being a good Church basketball player. I dreamed of going to the all-Church basketball tournament. But I never did. Finally my basketball dream came to an end, but not until it had given me great service. It had kept me going on an athletic program that made me a better man.

I don't feel sorry for those who don't realize all their dreams. I only feel sorry for those who don't have any dreams, who don't ever imagine that they're going to be in some significant way a special person.

One thing we all have to do with our dreams is to revise them from time to time. If we don't realize a dream, at least it got us through for a time. We can then revise it and get through some more hard spots. But some of our dreams will come true. At least enough of our dreams will come true that it will cause us to become special.

Dreams can also motivate us to try to be good at things even though self-doubt tries to hold us back. At college I decided I wanted to be an artist. At first I didn't know much about art and my work was pretty mediocre. But I *dreamed* that I was going to paint a great painting. I painted some paintings but they never were the ones I'd seen in my dreams. I still dream that someday, when I have more time, I'm going to take my canvas and my brushes again and paint that painting that only exists in my dreams. That dream brings me joy and makes me feel special.

I'll always remember my feeling of inadequacy as I departed on my mission. But I'd studied about Heber C. Kimball and I'd dreamed that I was going to be as he was. I dreamed that I'd bring thousands into the Church. I went out into the mission field with that idea, and all during my mission I dreamed about it. That dream caused me to struggle to find people to teach and to teach them by the Spirit. Wanting to be another Heber C. Kimball made me into a far better George D. Durrant. I still have the dream that someday, in some way, I'm going to be the Lord's instrument in bringing thousands into the Church. And that dream also brings me joy and makes me feel special.

I'm glad this chapter follows the one about feeling

inferior and the pain that often comes from that feeling, because I believe dreaming is one of the best remedies for such hurts. I don't mean fantasying about something that has no connection with reality, things such as flying like Superman. But I mean dreaming of things that are just barely possible.

I suppose that some of the dreams I'm describing could also be called hopes. Hope is a feeling you can have that soon something good is going to happen to you. Maybe it will happen tomorrow; if not tomorrow, then the next day; and if not on that day, then next week, or next month, or by Christmas, or next summer, but surely sometime. That kind of a dream and that kind of a hopeful feeling can bring great zest into your life.

When you are faced with your frustration and insecurity, you can either become negative and unwilling to try or you can dream a dream that will help you pull yourself loose from things that hold you back. You can gird up your loins and head out toward your dream.

So have a plentiful supply of dreams. Some of those dreams ought to show you a vision of things a bit beyond anything you think you might accomplish unless some really good things happen. In the back of your mind, deep down, have a feeling that you're going to see such dreams come true. If you have such feelings, your inward star—your real self—is already breaking through its dark clouds and its light is beginning to illuminate everything; and you are becoming special.

Chapter 4
Something Special Within Your Heart

I was one of the most spoiled children in my town and part of my tactics for getting my own way was my talent for crying. Though I felt inferior in many ways, I felt that in crying I was among the very best. When I would come crying to my mother about the persecution heaped upon me by my older brothers and their friends, she would call the other children in and say something such as: "You kids should quit teasing George. He's not the baby. You kids are babies." When she would say that I would stick my head out from behind her and say, "That's right!"

Once when I was playing with my older brother and some of his friends they told me to go in the house because I was too little to play the games they were playing. Heartbroken, I ran as quickly as I could to my mother. She heard my sobs, but on this day my mother didn't use her normal tactic of calling the others in for a rebuke.

She was making bread at the time, and she now took a large piece of dough and rolled it out flat with a rolling pin. When it was flat, she cut it up into pieces about the size of the palm of my hand and she started to fry it in some hot grease. She was making scones, and scones are good.

The sight and smell of the browning scones was enough to make me quit crying. I wondered why she was making so many. I knew that I couldn't eat but a small portion of them. She seemed to be making dozens. Finally she handed me the pan heaped to overflowing and said: "Take these scones. Go back outside and see if those other kids will play with you now."

I went outside and suddenly my whole world was changed. I had instant friends. I heard remarks such as: "Could I have a scone?" "What do you want to play now?" "Give me another one." "You can be the captain." "Can I have another scone?" "You can play any position you want." "How about one more?"

It was wonderful. I really had it made. I was popular. And as long as those scones lasted, I was the king of the neighborhood. But suddenly and sadly the scones were gone. With their disappearance things returned to normal, and the games and the other children drifted away and I was alone again.

From that experience I learned a great lesson: if you want to be popular, carry a pan of scones with you. If you do this the kids at school will say, "Here he comes, open the door for him. Hi, friend, could I have a scone? I'll vote for you; give me a scone."

I feel bad to have built up your hopes about how to be popular. For now it is my sad duty to burst this bubble by telling you that it won't work. You can't carry scones to school, because either they are gone quickly or they become cold and greasy and nobody really wants them.

But the scone story does hold the answer to our being special in the eyes of others and of ourselves. We can't carry a pan filled with scones, but we can fill our own hearts with a kind of inward scone that will make us most desirable. Then people will be attracted to us.

Yes, having scones in your heart is the answer, but doing so is not an easy task. Scones in the heart don't just come because you can play basketball, or wrestle, or play football, or act on the stage, or win in debate. Scones in the heart don't come because of a pretty face or figure, or a handsome frame. Scones in the heart are not something which come automatically, but they are something that through effort and deep desire can come to all of us.

As a mission president, I once had a long talk with one of my missionaries. He told me some interesting things about his high school days. In many ways his story reminded me of my own. It seems that this elder, like me, had been rather small of frame when he was going to school, but because he had a positive attitude he was one of the leaders of the school. When he became a ninth-grader he had as his dearest friend the biggest fellow in the school. My missionary's friend had unusual athletic ability. He could grip a basketball in one of his massive hands and hold it with his hand on top of the ball. (I've always considered that a real mark of success.) He could act as if the basketball was a baseball and he was going to throw it, yet he would hold on to it. He could hold it out in front of himself in one hand and tell you to hit it and see if you could knock it out of his hand. He had broad shoulders. Among his other claims to fame, he could throw a football with pinpoint accuracy over long distances. In the little town it was said of this husky ninth-grader, "When he gets to be in senior high, we'll win the state championship in both basketball and football."

My missionary and this fellow were bosom buddies.

28

They went everywhere together and they dreamed together about the future. They imagined that someday they would be the stars of their school's football and basketball teams.

My missionary told me that he recalled a time when he and his friend were in the ninth grade and they went on a camping trip. At night they were in their sleeping bags looking up at the stars and were talking seriously. As you know, in the right place at the right time ninth-graders can get into some quite deep discussions. They were talking of the future.

As they talked, the large boy said, "I'm going to give my whole heart and soul to athletics. I love this town. I want to bring them a championship. I love this school. I want to bring honors to the school." And then he vowed to my missionary: "I promise you I will give my heart and soul to athletics. I shall never smoke, and I shall never drink, and I shall obey every rule the coach ever sets down, because I want to see our school win."

My missionary said he had never been so touched by the words of another human being. And being caught up in the same spirit, he said to his bigger friend, "I too promise these things, for I too love the town, and the people, and the school, and I too will keep all the rules which are laid down for athletes." The two of them, under the stars, reached out and shook hands. This positive talk of two young men caused both to feel a great warmth in their hearts.

Because each lived on a farm and had chores to do, during the summer between the ninth and the tenth grades the two boys didn't see one another. When the school year began, they met in the halls of the school. My missionary, full of enthusiasm for the new year, shouted with great gusto to his friend, "What classes are you taking?" He was rather surprised to hear his friend say, "I don't know what to take. I don't even want to go to school." The missionary, somewhat surprised, announced: "I'm taking shop and gym and seminary and all the good classes. Why don't you take them?" The big athletic-looking sophomore replied, "I'm not taking shop." He then added in a bitter tone: "That teacher hates my guts. And he's not alone. All the teachers around this crummy school have got it in for me."

Shocked at these words, my missionary replied: "They haven't got it in for you. Where did you get that idea?" The friend said in disgust: "Never mind where I got the idea. I know what I know, and if I could I'd drop out of school. The only thing that keeps me here is my parents. I'd like to get out of here and clear out of this town."

My missionary told me that he couldn't understand what had happened to his friend. He said that he noticed that some of the other guys had changed too. They looked about the same, except that they were a bit more mature. The difference was that some who had been quite positive in their attitudes had become sort of negative.

It was only a week or so later when the coach told the boys in P.E. class that after school all those interested in playing football should come to the gym. At that time he would announce who had made the football team. There would only be ten sophomores on the team because the remainder of the positions on the junior varsity team were filled with older boys.

My missionary told me that he went there with his friend and they stood together while the coach appeared with his all-important list. As the coach would read a name he would then issue the shoulder pads, the hip pads, the cleats and other football gear. It took some time to do this. He called the first boy's name and took the time to give him the various pieces of gear. My missionary's friend had supposed that he would be the first called, and when he wasn't he became rather irritated. After five boys' names had been called, the friend's name still hadn't been. He became disgusted at this point and said he was leaving. He told the missionary who was telling me the story: "Tell the coach that if he wants me to play football I'll be out in the hall. He can come and get me."

The next name called was the friend's name, but he wasn't there. The coach looked around, then looked at my missionary and said, "Where is he?" My missionary replied, "He had to step out in the hall." "Go find him," the coach shouted. "Tell him if he wants to play football to get back here."

The missionary found his friend and told him that the coach had called his name and wanted him to come back. And at that, this fine potential athlete made this statement: "You tell the coach to go to hell." The missionary went back and told the coach, "He said he can't come back right now." And the coach said, "If he doesn't come back within the next few minutes, he's not going to play football."

The missionary went and pleaded with his friend to come back, but he wouldn't. Those broad shoulders never did feel shoulder pads, and those big hands never did throw a football for the school.

As my missionary finished his story, tears came to his eyes as he added, "And we never did win the championship." He continued, "In gym classes my friend would surpass any of the guys who were on the football team. But they had something he didn't. They had desire and a positive attitude and he didn't. He had the size and great ability. But size and ability never will be as important as attitude. Because he had become bitterly negative, my friend gave up positive activities that could have created memories which would have been dear to him forever."

My missionary concluded this sad tale by adding: "As our school career unfolded, this fellow remained in school but he would often go to a place where he could smoke and do other things he shouldn't have. He idled away his time while he anxiously awaited the day when, as he had said, he could 'get out of that crummy school.' Some of the other young people were attracted to him because they too wanted to go contrary to the positive way. But the kind of people he attracted were people just like himself, miserable people, people who were fighting against the very things that could have made them happy."

It doesn't matter how big or small we are; we have the power to be in our heart what we want to be. The way we feel in our heart is indeed the barometer of just how special we are.

Feeling good or positive inside is almost as difficult as scaling a high, steep cliff. As we grow up and our bodies begin to change from that of a child into that of a man or woman, the process brings with it certain stresses and strains which often seem to draw us emotionally toward disagreeable feelings. To drift toward a negative attitude seems the natural course if one just lets oneself go. But special people need not be victims of this current. We all know friends who are able to fight against the inclination to be sour and disgruntled. They remain positive throughout their years. Each of us at times feels a bit negative. Therefore we should strive with all our hearts to stay positive and pleasant. And as we struggle to keep good feelings in our heart we begin to fill our heart with delicious ''scones,'' and people then desire our company.

I know a man whose son was one of the most unusual and choice young men who ever lived. He had stored so many scones in his heart that it was a joy to know him. His warm smile and cheerful greeting caused many to love him. He knew how to goof off, but never in such a way that anybody got hurt. He knew how to have fun, but it was always clean fun. As the school years went by, he attracted many friends because of his positive and sincere attitude. In his last year of high school he was elected senior class president. But toward the end of that year, this fine young man, who had never been sick in his life, contracted a rare disease. Within a period of just ten days he had gone from perfect health to death.

This was a heartbreaking experience for all who knew him, but particularly for his father. This father was aware that his son was a most unusual young man, and the two of them, as well as being father and son, had been the dearest of friends. The father didn't know how he could carry on after sustaining the loss of this boy who had been so much the pride and love of his heart.

The night before the funeral, many people called at the mortuary, and one by one they tried to say those words that might bring comfort. But it seemed that the father couldn't be comforted. Finally there came a young man who was regarded by the other students as a social misfit. This boy, who was a loner, had very few friends. He had some problems that he hadn't brought upon himself but which limited him socially. As this awkward young man stood before the father he was not able to use any eloquent words whereby to offer any comfort.

He stood silently on that sacred ground and looked into the father's eyes. Then he began to sob. Amidst his sobs he was able to utter these words: "The only reason I ever came to school was because of your son. Every time I saw him in the hall he smiled, he stopped, and he talked to me. He made me feel that I was really somebody. He's the only one in the school who ever did that. Now that he's gone, I don't know if I can even keep coming to school. He was the only friend I've ever had." These words pierced the very heart of the father, and he and the social misfit fell into one another's arms and wept together. To a greater degree than had been the case in many days, the father was comforted.

One of life's dearest blessings is that of knowing somebody who has positive feelings within himself which enable him to reach out and help one and all with equal respect. An example of such a person was another young man who won the school election and became the student body president. As he arrived home that evening, his mother, seeing that he was downhearted, said, "Oh, my son, you lost the election, didn't you?"

He replied, "No, Mom, I won. But my best friend lost, and he feels terrible. I wish he could have won, because it hurts me to know how he feels."

Then there was the young man who was one of the most popular people in the school. He learned that a certain girl had never had a date to a school dance. Much to the dismay of several other girls, he asked this girl to go with him. Thus he made her a Cinderella, because he was indeed a "prince."

When you come to be like these young men, and

34

when you have those kind of feelings in your heart, your heart becomes filled with scones. Then it doesn't matter so much how tall you are or how short or how thin or how graceful or how athletic. There's just something there that people see with eyes that might be described as spiritual eyes. People start to say of you, "He cares." You thus develop a deep and sincere personality. And when you do, people gather around you and say, "What do you want to play now?" "Could I just be with you?" It's as though you are able to take scones from your heart and give one to everybody, and yet you never run out.

Scones made of dough and fried to a light brown are delicious, but there's something far, far better; something that doesn't just tickle the taste buds, but something that thrills the heart of others and of yourself. And that something is a loving, caring, positive attitude. These feelings are the "scones of the heart." When we have these things in our heart, those who know us best love us most.

So of all your journeys and all your quests, none will be as important as a daily effort to fight off negative feelings—feelings of saying negative things about teachers, schools, towns, or parents; feelings which would lead you to say that you will be glad when this crummy experience is over or when you get out of this mess.

Nobody can fight this battle of negative versus positive attitudes for you. It's up to you to send an army of positive feelings inside yourself to kick out any negative feelings that try to find a home there. Pray for the strength to be positive; and as you do, into your heart will flow those positive things which will indeed make you feel special. Your happiness or misery is determined by your own attitude. And when your attitude is special, the whole world is special.

Chapter 5
To Be Destiny-Bound Is a Special Feeling

Someone said to me just after I reached my fortieth birthday, "What are you going to be when you grow up?" I replied, "I don't know, I just want to grow up." I believe growing up is more important than what you're going to be when you grow up. Growing up, as I define it here, is to become special. I don't mean that you can't be special as you grow up, but the thing that makes you special as you grow up is the fact that you want to grow to be somebody really special.

Some, looking ahead to when they will be grown up, want to be doctors; others desire to be professional ball players; others long to be school teachers; others farmers; and so on and on. Seeing in your mind what you desire to work at is a blessing to those who can do it; but if, while you are in high school or even into the early years of college, you don't know what profession you want to go into, or what vocation you want to pursue, it doesn't have to be a cause for major concern.

Your destiny is realized only in part by what you choose to do for a living. The mainstream of your destiny comes as you do those things that put scones in your heart and make you the kind of person who has character and who cares about others. Your divine destiny, reduced to its simplest form, is to become somebody special.

To Be Destiny-Bound Is a Special Feeling

When you feel yourself going toward that destiny it gives you a special inward feeling. People are attracted to those who are actively building themselves into a better person, people who seem to know what they want and who are destiny bound.

As we discussed previously, many of us in our younger years suffer from feelings of inferiority. We wonder how we fit in. We wonder how we compare with others. To help ourselves along we dream in our mind and heart of the time when we will be a movie star, a popular singer, a race-car driver, a rodeo champion, or the governor of the state. Along with these lofty and legitimate dreams, we ought to have a quiet little dream wherein we just long to be good. This very reachable dream is in reality the dream that best portrays our destiny.

We might not want to announce this dream to everyone. There are some who might ridicule us a little if they heard that one of our goals was just to be good. The dream to be good is one that could be kept to oneself or shared with only dearest friends. Part of such a dream is a desire to be perfectly honest, perfectly loyal in our friendships, perfectly willing to help those who are in need, perfectly true to our Heavenly Father. With these kinds of dreams we can quietly move, day by day, toward our destiny. The Lord will help us fulfill such a dream, for this is exactly the desire that he has for us.

When I was in the ninth grade and my mother told me I was special, I sort of thought she was right. But at the same time I had decided in my mind that I couldn't do anything very well. I felt that other students didn't really look upon me as being special. As a result of these feelings, I gained a deep fear of standing before groups of people. I was afraid they might laugh at me or that in some way I might make a fool of myself. As a result, I did all I could to avoid being in front of a group and having them look at me. This fear even affected my basketball playing. The crowd would cause me to choke up because I was fearful that I might not play as well as I should. I had little confidence, and a ball player without confidence is like a light without electricity.

In one of my classes I sat at the back. I would put my feet under the chair in front of me and slump down in my seat as far as I could. I wasn't very big, and in this way I could almost disappear. That is exactly what I often felt like doing. I felt that I was not on my way to anything. I was not destiny bound. My inner self told me that my mother was right—"I am special," "I should be doing better in school, I should stand up and do things, I should be a leader." But the world about me seemed to suggest that I retreat into my own inner shell where there was more safety.

Every Friday in this particular class it was the practice of the teacher to allow those who desired to do so to give a report on current events. As she called the roll 'at the beginning of class she expected one of two responses from each of us. When she called out our names we could either answer "Prepared" (which meant that we were ready and willing to give a talk) or "Unprepared" (which meant that we were not prepared to talk). Because I was a bright young man I quickly figured out this system. I found that I could avoid these talks by using the word *unprepared*. My friends in the class also used this word. We supported each other as supposed friends do.

Those who said "prepared" had to give a talk, while we who said "unprepared" didn't ever have to move. But we weren't just idle, because we caused a little trouble in the back of the room by sometimes laughing just a little. This made the person giving the talk aware that we were making fun of him or her. Perhaps this is why I was fearful of speaking. I could not bear to have anyone laugh at me.

Week after week went by, and each Friday when the teacher would call my name, "George," I would answer "Unprepared." I knew that my long list of "unprepareds" would be the raw material for an "F" on my report card. I didn't want to take such a grade home to my parents, but to me that was easier than risking my almost dead pride in front of the class. So I kept saying "Unprepared." I even imagined that I got so that I could say it with quite a bit of dignity. But now I know that the word *unprepared* can never be said with dignity.

In the class was a girl I liked. I liked her as much as a ninth-grader can like a girl; and, as I recall, that's quite a bit. I liked her to the point where I didn't even dare talk to her, let alone really express myself to her about my feelings. She was one of those who had both a pretty face and "scones in her heart." She was one of those who seemed to care about everyone. But she seemed to care about me in a special way. Sometimes in my dreams I imagined that she was in love with me. What she said meant a great deal to me.

One Friday as the teacher was calling the roll, she called the name "George." In my usual way, I said "Un-prepared." At that time, to my surprise this girl turned around and stared at me. I quickly looked away from her, but I knew she was looking at me, because you can tell when people are looking at you. I looked first to one side and then to the other. But she waited me out until, not knowing where else to look, I looked fully into her eyes.

39

As I did so, she spoke with firmness, "Why don't you get prepared?" Then she turned away.

Her words seemed to explode into my heart. For a time I couldn't even think. As I began to calm down I found myself wondering, "What does *she* care, unless she cares." All day long I thought about what she had said. You know how our minds work; yours is always working, and so is mine—thinking thoughts, ever thinking thoughts, all sorts of thoughts.

That night I clipped an article from the newspaper and began to memorize it. Finally I had done just that. Every word was in my mind. The great accomplishment of memorizing that much material was not made easier by my rather average ability to memorize. But intelligence always has been tempered greatly by desire and motivation, and I was now motivated by the very force that makes the world go around. Finally, when I knew I had every word memorized, I folded the paper neatly and put it in my wallet and carried it with me all the week.

When the next Friday arrived I was sitting up a little straighter because this was a different kind of a day. The teacher was at the front with her roll book. (I had seen this roll earlier, when I had visited with her. As you know, some students get to visit with the teacher more than others do.) It was her habit to put a negative sign by the names of each who answered "Unprepared," and a positive sign by the names of the prepared. When I had seen the roll book a week or so earlier I noticed that on the line headed by the name *George Durrant* there was a long row of negative signs. These negative signs seemed an accurate appraisal of the way things were going for me. But this day was different.

The teacher was calling the roll. She didn't look up,

because if a teacher does that she gets the marks on the wrong line. Finally she got down to the D's. I heard the word "George." There was a brief second or so of silence, and then I softly responded, "Prepared." The teacher stopped calling the roll and looked down to where I sat. I nodded my head up and down. She looked amazed. My friends all looked over at me as if to say, "You traitor!" The girl turned around and looked into my eyes and smiled.

But now the glory was over, and I wondered, "What in the world have I done? What have I said?" For I knew that by saying "Prepared" I had committed myself to get up and perform. Only those whose insecurities equaled mine can imagine how I felt.

I found myself wishing that I hadn't said it. Time raced right at me as one by one the other prepared students gave their talks. Now it was my turn. The teacher looked down to where I sat, and I knew that it was an invitation to come forward. I somehow made my way to the front. I took a deep breath, lifted my head, and looked out at my fellow students. To my relief I found that they weren't laughing. They were all looking up at me in complete amazement as if they could not believe what they were seeing.

I started to speak. I remembered the first word, the first sentence, the first paragraph. I remembered every word of the entire article. Desiring to be truthful at the risk of being boastful, I feel compelled to say that that was the finest talk ever given at American Fork Junior High.

When I had finished speaking, and as I was still momentarily standing there in front of the class, there surged through my body and my soul a thought that hadn't been there for quite a while. For into my heart and into my mind came the simple thought, *"George, I like you!"* I have since come to cherish that above all other thoughts. It is such a thought that makes us able to believe the words, "I am indeed a child of God and I am special."

As I made my way back to my seat I had an added courage. I looked down at the girl and we exchanged smiles. I then collapsed into my seat and found myself thinking, "This is the only way to live."

That day in the roll book the teacher, out of habit, first put a minus or a negative sign by my name. But when I said "Prepared" she added a vertical line that made a plus or positive sign by my name. The memory of that thrills me. Why, that's the highest of all marks! To have a plus by your name is an honor of the greatest magnitude.

I can't say that school was easy for me after that, but from time to time I caught a brief glimpse of my destiny. I knew it wasn't for me to slump down in the back of the room. I knew it was my destiny to get up and do something; to get up and let George Durrant have a chance to be what he was supposed to be. Not a dud, not somebody who couldn't do anything, but somebody, even though frightened, who would stand up and do something good. I found that there is an exhilarating feeling that comes when one catches a vision of his destiny and feels that he is progressing toward that destiny by some little thing that he is doing today. I found that it is a joy to move forward against the current of fear and do difficult things.

Happiness comes in encouraging others to do the same. Remember that others feel like you do, and we all need a little moral support. Be like the girl in my class. Turn around and say to a fellow who needs encouragement,

"Why don't you get prepared?" Don't ever do things that discourage others from being destiny bound. Sometimes people are just starting to come out of their shell. Their flame is like the flame of a match. It can easily be blown out. Don't blow it out—add fuel and help it burn. Much of life's very purpose is to do what you can to encourage and aid other people. As you do these things you are making the journey toward your destiny of being a special person.

The Book of Mormon records the story of Jared and his brother. They were in the land where the tower of Babel was being built. In order to stop this foolish project, the Lord confounded the tongues and the languages of the people. Through the prayers of Jared's brother, he and Jared, their families and friends received a special favor from the Lord and their language was not confounded. They were also told by the Lord that they would be led to the most choice land on earth (America).

They left the tower of Babel and wandered for some time until they reached a goodly land on the shores of the sea. But they had not yet reached the promised land. It appears that the place that they were in was such a beautiful land and such an easy place to live in that with little effort they became quite satisfied. After three years of living in this land, which was an ocean away from the promised land, the Lord spoke to the brother of Jared and asked him why he had not remembered to pray.

It seems strange to think that this mighty man who had had such great faith in the past had given up prayer. Some have supposed that he hadn't really quit praying, but rather that he had stopped moving toward his destiny. He had become content to live in a land that wasn't the land of promise. He was living in a land that we could call "Rutville." It was an easy place to live in. It was there

44

that the brother of Jared and the others had found a comfortable, unstressful life. It appears likely that the brother of Jared was still saying his prayers, but he wasn't praying with the intense pleading desire of someone who wants to move forward toward his destiny.

After the divine rebuke, the brother of Jared repented. He went to the Lord with his former enthusiasm for prayer. He asked how he could build barges and how he could get light in them. In his prayer he answered the Lord's challenge to move on with the word *prepared*.

As the brother of Jared moved toward his destiny, the Lord himself appeared to him. He saw the Lord face to face! He hadn't seen the Lord while he was sitting back, comfortably slumping in his chair, so to speak. He didn't have his great vision until he decided to move forward in the face of difficulty.

So it is with you. When you are willing to get up and give a speech, be in a roadshow, play ball for the Church team, ask a girl who doesn't go to every dance to go to this one with you, take some person by the hand and let him or her know that you care, give a talk in church, help a teacher who is almost ready to give up because the kids give him such a bad time, try to create a better atmosphere in the locker room where perhaps there is a lot of swearing or dirty jokes—when you do such things, you too can come to feel the Lord's presence in your life. As we do these kinds of things we have the thrill of moving toward our destiny. And such a movement gives us a special feeling.

I think my friend Mike, whom we've discussed in earlier chapters, was starting to get that special kind of a feeling as he and I had many long talks and as he started to do positive things. At one point I was invited to a youth conference in Provo. I was at the time living in Salt Lake City, which was Mike's home town. I told him that I was going to the conference and that I wanted him to be my companion there. He seemed genuinely thrilled and said that he would like that. It appeared that he was finally beginning to catch the vision of his destiny and was willing to take the steps that would lead him forward. We arranged that early on Sunday morning I would pick him up at his apartment and we would drive to the youth conference.

I prepared that talk as I had prepared no other. I was to speak to the youth of a stake from Colorado, but mainly I was going to speak to Mike. I was going to talk about the things that would help him.

I got an early start that morning and drove to Mike's apartment. I knocked on the door, but there was no answer. I pounded on the door. No one responded. Finally someone from next door asked, "Who are you looking for?" I replied, "Mike." The person said, "He left yesterday in his car headed for California with a couple of his friends." I couldn't believe what I was hearing. I had been certain that he would be ready to go with me. As I walked back to my car I was bitterly disappointed.

Driving to Provo, I couldn't get Mike off my mind. As I spoke at the conference, I told the youth about Mike. I could hardly keep from crying as I did so. Because of him I was able to touch the hearts of my listeners, but not his. I feel that if he had been there with me that morning Mike's whole life would have been different. But instead he went in another direction.

It wasn't until three days later that I heard from him. He called me, saying that he was out of money and that his friends had abandoned him. His car was out of gas and he was stranded. He wanted to know if I could do anything to get him some money so that he could return to Salt Lake City. I told him that his only hope was to contact a bishop down there. There he was, five hundred miles further away from his destiny than he had been just a few days before.

What a difference a little decision can make! I'm almost of the opinion that there aren't any big decisions, just little ones. Our day-by-day decisions cause us to move either toward our destiny or away from it. As you make a decision to meet a situation by saying "Prepared," something comes into your heart that makes you feel special. When that happens, life is altogether different. You get a plus sign by your name. Many plus signs added together cause you to have a positive attitude. The name of Christ becomes written in your heart.

When everything else has been stripped away, all that will really matter is: "Were the feelings of your heart positive or were they negative? Were you prepared or unprepared? Did you move toward or away from your destiny?"

Being destiny-bound is a special journey. And as you go forth one step at a time you will feel and you will be special.

Chapter 6
If It Is to Be
It Is up to Me

By using these ten two-letter words, "If it is to be it is up to me," someone portrayed to us a mighty truth. You can say, "I have little chance to be special because my parents are divorced," or "because we aren't a wealthy family," or "because I have a sub-standard environment," or "because other circumstances have come upon me." But such statements, although they often describe a tremendous force, are not real deterrents to your becoming special. Your being special or not being special is not determined by your environment. It's determined by you. I know it is hard for some to accept this, but it is a divine truth. And until you accept it, you cannot push aside the dark clouds that keep you from being special. Because they are the children of God, all men have the power to rise up and be what they are potentially destined to become.

I recall being called to Kentucky and Tennessee as a mission president. My son Matt was at the time a ninth-grader in a Salt Lake City school. There he had made many friends and had enjoyed an excellent social life. His keen sense of humor and other characteristics had helped him find satisfaction at school. It was my lot to advise him that this pleasant life with its comfortable environment was to change.

I chose as the place for this news conference with my son a local restaurant—a place where you could go through the line and get all the food you wanted. After we had gone through the line and were sitting at the table, the only way I could see him was to look around the masses of food that balanced precariously on his plate.

After our prayer, and just as he started to eat, I broke the news. He was of course shocked, but as he swallowed the food he was eating, he said: "I'm ready to go, Dad. I'm proud of you, and I'll do my best." I don't think he realized then, and nor did I, how difficult the years ahead would be for him.

We arrived in Kentucky just in time for him to start his sophomore year in the largest school in the state. His only acquaintances were three or four other Mormon young people whom he had met a week or so earlier in church. As the first few weeks passed by he got right into his studies, and his grades appeared to be excellent. But his social life suffered. He didn't feel that he belonged there. He had no real friends. Although he didn't discuss this with me, he spent many, many anxious days wishing he was back with his old friends.

He became depressed. But he had hope, because it would soon be time for the basketball team to be chosen. He was certain that this would be the doorway to happiness. He made the junior varsity team but often found himself seated on the bench. Although he was good, he was not yet as good as he had dreamed he might be. So basketball, his last hope, was not giving him the satisfaction he needed. His sophomore year was not a happy one.

Then came the beginning of his junior year. He had grown considerably and had practiced basketball all summer. Many at the school had gained respect for him because of his straight "A" grades, an unusual thing on that particular basketball team. He had some satisfaction in that, but he wanted satisfaction along different lines. He wanted social satisfaction and athletic satisfaction. He felt that he had to prove himself. To him, the place to do that was on the basketball court.

The time came for the varsity team to be chosen. He had played well and was hoping to be on the main five. He enthusiastically entered the gymnasium to look at that all-important list posted by the coach. He stood with others looking at the names. He read from top to bottom. His name was not on the list at all. He had been cut from the team. In his mind that meant he had been cut from everything.

He returned home that day before school was out, went to his room and stayed there. I knew of the deep grief he was suffering but didn't know how to help. On the second day of his sorrows, late at night I went downstairs to his room. His light was still on and he was looking up at the ceiling from his position lying on the bed. We talked. We talked for a long time. He told me of his deep sorrow and wondered if he could ever return to school. He told me that he had prayed and asked the Lord to help him make the team. And now he said, "I've prayed for strength." But there seemed to be no help and there seemed to be no hope. I thought my heart would break as I saw my son suffer. I listened, I loved, and I silently prayed.

After a while he said to me: "Dad, I'm just going to have to start over. I'm going to have to build on something else. I know no one else can do it for me. I've got to do it for myself." With tear-filled eyes he said to me, "Dad, I want to be like Elder Jibson and I think I can be." He had

50

named one of the elders who was serving in the mission. He continued: "I'm going to be like him. I'm going to learn to smile like him, and to love and care like him. Dad, I'm going to make it. I'm going back to school and I'm going to start over." We knelt in prayer together, and then I told him of my love for him and of the great pride I had in him.

The next day he went to school. During that season he played basketball for the church team, where he was a star. He started to make many friends at school. He seemed to be relaxed, and he returned to and further developed his keen sense of humor. As time went by I heard him saying such things as: "Dad, these guys are great! I love this school. I love this town and I love Kentucky. I even wonder if after our mission we could live here."

The beginning of his senior year arrived. Because of some difficulties in the school system they had not yet elected the student body president for the year. He decided to run for president. By now he had many friends. He carried on a great campaign based on positive, fun-loving things about how he could help the school to be a better place. He was elected by a landslide. Of course, he was thrilled.

But there was one last dream at his school and that was something he hadn't been able to get out of his system. He wanted to be on the basketball team. The coach had announced that he wouldn't carry any seniors who hadn't played as juniors. Instead he wanted juniors on the team who could help him in the future. Thus there seemed to be no hope for Matt, who was a senior. Nevertheless he practiced long and hard, and the guys who were the stars on the team came to love and respect him.

51

When the list was posted, once again his name did not appear. As much as he had tried to build himself in other directions, he was again heartbroken. He came home and told me of his problems. At the time I was just departing on a journey and I wouldn't return for five days. All that I could do while I was gone was pray.

When I got back I found that Matt was not home. He was at basketball practice. I inquired if he was practicing with the church and I was told that he was practicing with the school. About that time he arrived home. "How come you practice with the team?" I asked. "You told me you were cut."

"Well, Dad," he replied, "the guys on the team all went to the coach and told him they wanted me on the team. The coach did something he'd never done before. He put me on the team because the guys said 'We need Matt.' They convinced the coach, so I'm on the team."

He continued his friendly ways. School was composed of both blacks and whites. He befriended them all. He became a great influence in the school—to help unify it, to help all to have more pride in it. On one occasion in a senior class meeting there arose a division among the black students and the white students over who should play the music at the last dance. The blacks wanted a black group and the whites wanted a certain white group. Some of the more vocal groups of both factions began to shout, and a potential little riot seemed to be shaping up. Matt got the microphone.

"Quiet, quiet," he said. And then when there was silence he continued. "I have a solution. There's a group up in Cincinnati we can get. It's five Chinese guys."

His announcement was first met with silence, but then

came a unanimous burst of laughter. Tempers cooled and a sensible discussion followed.

Matt and the other Mormon kids, as a group, set a great example at that school. A Mormon girl became vice president and she was also named Miss Seneca, the highest honor the school could bestow upon a young lady.

Matt still felt bad about basketball because he was usually on the bench. One night at a team meeting the projector broke down and game films could not be shown as planned. The team and the coach just sat around and talked. Matt sort of entertained the group. For the first time the coach really found out who Matt was. In the next game he played for over half the game. From then on he was a major factor in many games and gained recognition as a superior athlete.

Finally it was graduation time. He was chosen to give one of the talks. The humor in the talk caused a good deal of laughter. But it was also a serious talk. Toward the conclusion of his remarks, he spoke of the joy he had known there—the warmth of the people, the love he had for the other students. He closed by saying: "My dear friends, in a few days my parents and I will be returning to Utah. As you know, I am a Mormon. I conclude my remarks by using the unforgettable words of a great Mormon prophet Brigham Young. His words describe my feeling. I love all of you because of the way you've treated me and the happiness and joy I've had here. And so I say to you, as he once said, "This is the place." The students and the public rose to their feet and gave him a standing ovation.

Matt had made many steps toward his destiny, a journey which started in a quiet room where, after a trial of his faith, he made a decision to start over, a decision which could be paraphrased by the words, "If it is to be it is up to me." He had decided to build first upon the idea of reaching his destiny as a special person. As he did that, other things fell into place.

In speaking to his sons, one noble father in Book of Mormon times gave the greatest advice he could give them:

"And now, my sons, remember, remember that it is upon the rock of our Redeemer, who is Christ, the son of God, that ye must build your foundation; that when the devil shall send forth his mighty winds, yea, his shafts in the whirlwind, yea, when all his hail and his mighty storm shall beat upon you, it shall have no power over you to drag you down to the gulf of misery and endless wo, because of the rock upon which ye are built, which is a sure foundation, a foundation whereon if men build they cannot fall." (Helaman 5:12.)

Make a decision to let all your decisions be made in the light of becoming a special person, a person who loves his fellowmen and loves the Lord. Pick out a model who seems to have a special spirit. Try to be like that person. Ask yourself what he or she would do in your shoes. Keep in mind *he* who was perfect and try to be like him. Build your life upon the Savior, Jesus Christ. If you do, you cannot fall. Basketball lists may not include your name. The honors of men might not be heaped upon you. But those who know you will trust you, will love you, and will look upon you as special.

Chapter 7
Put Your Hand into the Hand of God

My young son once asked me to tell him a story. "I will," I said. "I'll tell you a story from the Bible." I told him of how David, the young man who defeated a giant, picked up the stone from the brook and hurled it with his sling. I explained how the stone pierced the giant's forehead and the giant fell. He seemed thrilled as he realized that young David had won.

I then asked my son this question: "How could a young man face an enemy giant, and win?" He didn't answer immediately, so I decided to help him. I said, "Did he win because Heavenly Father was with him?" He thought for a few seconds and then said: "No, Dad, he didn't need Heavenly Father. He had a sling."

The boy was very young at the time and he had made a mistake in replying. But it was a mistake of the kind that has been made millions of times by millions of people. He had mistakenly supposed that if you've got your own sling you don't need the help of the Lord. Those who make this error feel that they have so many things going for them that they can make it quite well by themselves. On the other hand, there are those who feel that they have no sling at all and who have the feeling: "What does God care about me? I've got nothing to offer. I'm not going to be anything special. Therefore I don't need the Lord and he surely doesn't need or even want me."

The person who does have a "sling," or much natural talent, has a potential to make a great contribution. But he will never make the fulness of that contribution unless he puts his hand into the hand of God. He might do well, but he won't do at all what he might have done had he been magnified by the Lord. And the person who feels that he doesn't have anything special to offer to anyone can find out by putting his hand into the hand of God that indeed he has a most special gift to give.

Religion is more than it appears to be when you're young. It can do something within your heart that makes you feel special. Religion is not just going to church, although it includes that; it's a feeling deep down inside that you are a partner with God and you're trying to live the way he would want you to live. You don't always have to be trying to prove you're the most religious guy in the school. Just quietly keep your standards. Speak in such a way that people know you don't swear or tell off-color jokes. Wear your religion in your heart and not as if it were a shirt that can be worn at times and removed at others. This will take great effort, for wearing your religion in your heart is often more difficult than mountain climbing. But God loves those who try, and as you pray to him he will make you equal to the task.

While I was growing up, my father raised white chickens. They laid white eggs. I bought some brown eggs and put them under a white setting hen. They hatched out as little brown chickens, and when they got big they laid brown eggs. We put my brown chickens in the coops with the white ones. I helped gather the eggs and take care of the chickens. The pay for my labors was brown eggs—all the brown eggs laid were mine. There were a couple of dozen a week, and I raised a little money by selling them.

This money gave me some popularity with my older brother and his friends because they had a 1931 model A Ford car, but they were seldom fortunate enough to have money to buy gas. They advised me that I could go with them any time I wanted to if I would provide the money for the gasoline. I felt kind of big as I rode around with these guys. They were all older than I was and were athletes as well. I thought it helped my prestige to ride around town with them in the Model A.

I remember waving to my friends as we passed them, and I suppose my friends were saying, "There goes old George—he's kind of a big wheel riding with those guys." So I thought my money was being well spent.

Week after week we'd go out in the Model A. During that period of time, I regularly attended church with my mother. There weren't too many young men in our ward, so my friend Herbie Pawloski and I blessed the sacrament every Sunday. I enjoyed blessing the sacrament. I'd kneel down at the table and try to read each word just right. As I did this, a good feeling would come into my heart. I also liked breaking the bread while the people sang the sacrament song. I'd softly sing along, and as I stood there helping the Lord I'd really feel special.

Each Sunday afternoon, I knew that my mother was expecting me to go to church and the bishop was expecting me to bless the sacrament. But one Sunday, a little while before the time for church, my brother and his friends came and told me that if I had some money they wanted me to go with them in the Model A. I did have some money. And I thought, "Because I've attended church so regularly in the past, perhaps today would be the time when I could miss."

Put Your Hand into the Hand of God

As I was about to get into the Model A, my mother asked me where I was going and I said I was going with the fellows. "Will you be back for church?" she asked, and I replied, "I don't think so." She looked hurt, but I got in the Model A and away we went. We rode around and had a good time. I thought from time to time about the fact that I ought to be in church. That sort of dampened the fun, but it sure was good to be with those big guys.

It so happened that we were driving past the church shortly after the meeting had ended, and the people were coming out. My mother was coming down the stairs all by herself. I wondered who would walk home with her and I wondered who had helped Herbie bless the sacrament. I wondered if the bishop had missed me.

Suddenly I found myself feeling very miserable. Tomorrow would be Monday and I would have to go back to school. The thought of going back to school on Monday always used to be something of a hard thought for me to face on Sunday night. I didn't dislike school, but it seemed as if Monday wasn't a very happy day and consequently I usually didn't feel happy anticipating it during the last hours of the weekend. But on this Sunday night, after the Model A ride was over and I was home again, I had a deep case of misery. I finally asked Mother who the bishop had asked to help Herbie bless the sacrament. She told me one of the men had. I sat silently for a time and then I said, "Mom, next week I'll be there." She smiled. Just saying that next week I'd be there made me feel better, and I started getting over my misery. The next week I was there.

Religion, then, is being there when the Lord needs you and then having the assurance that he'll be there when you need him. And we need him all the time, because he can help us feel special instead of miserable.

A few years later I got a job at a service station which sometimes required that I work on Sunday. I'd go to church every time I could, but sometimes I would have to miss sacrament meeting. I didn't yet know for sure that the Church was true, but I really thought it was. I'd go to sacrament meeting and the bishop would meet me at the door and shake hands with me and tell me how glad he was to see me. I liked him.

He would say, "George, would you like to give the closing prayer?" It seemed that every time I went to church he would say that. I used to sit there and think, "I wonder if anyone else in the church knows how to give the closing prayer?" Finally the closing song would be near the end of the last verse and I would walk to the front. I'd bow my head and offer the closing prayer. I'd get a special feeling as I stood there talking to the Lord. After I had offered such a prayer, ward members would come up to me and say, "That sure was a good closing prayer," and I'd think to myself, "You know, that really was a good prayer." I felt a special kind of thrill doing something for the Lord. It was not like making a basket in a basketball game, but in a different way it was even better.

Religion is kind of a partnership with the Lord. You try to find out what he wants you to do. To do this, you attend church, study the scriptures, listen carefully to your leaders and to your conscience. And as you strive to live his laws he helps you out and does things for you that you can't quite do for yourself.

I recall when, as a young man, I was called on a mission and went to the mission home in Salt Lake City. I thought I had brought everything they had asked me to bring. Late one afternoon, the mission home president said: "Tomorrow we go to the temple. Of course, all of

60

you have your temple recommends." It was then I remembered that I had forgotten mine. I became panicky in my soul. I thought, "When they find out that I forgot my recommend they will think that I didn't deserve to go on a mission and they'll send me home." I thought all sorts of things like that.

A little while later the meeting was dismissed and everyone was to go to the evening meal. But not me. I ran to downtown Salt Lake and found a phone booth. Phone calls were a nickel in those days. I looked in the phone book for the address of the Highway Patrol—my bishop was a highway patrolman. My finger tracked down the list, and finally I saw *Highway Patrol,* but to my chagrin there was not one but several numbers, and I didn't know which one to call.

There wasn't room in the phone booth to kneel down. Standing there, I just sort of called out within my soul, "Heavenly Father, I've got to find the right one, please help me." I ran my finger down the column and stopped where I felt impressed to stop. I put my nickel in and dialed. I said to the lady who answered, "I want to speak to Mel Grant." "How did you know he was here?" she asked, "I didn't know he was there," I told her, "but I just have to talk to him." "He hardly ever comes here," she said; but she added, "He's here now."

When my bishop said "hello" I knew I'd been saved. I told him my problem. Bishops are great ones to tell problems to. It's such a blessing to have a bishop. He told me not to worry, that he would head back to American Fork and get my recommend and have it brought to me by another highway patrolman who would be coming to Salt Lake City that night.

About three hours later I was in an auditorium with

all of the other missionaries. The meeting was in full progress when from the back, down the center aisle of the hall and up to the stand came a highway patrolman. He whispered something to the mission home president. The president stood, interrupted the speaker, and said, "This man would like to see Elder George Durrant." A hush fell over the whole congregation. I arose from my seat, all eyes upon me. I made my way to the aisle and followed the highway patrolman into the foyer. There he extended his hand, in which he held a small piece of paper. He gave me a ticket, a ticket to go to the temple. I have never had such a glorious ticket in all my life.

The Lord knew I had a problem and he took over and saved me. He doesn't always do things just that way, because sometimes we need to work things out for ourselves. But when we can't, and when something really needs to happen, and if it is for a good purpose, after we've done all we can he works it out for us. He sends us a little or a big miracle just often enough that we always know he's there. When we know he's there it gives us confidence.

Every young person would pray much more if he knew the kind of help that is available through prayer. When they go to a dance, some feel a need to drink so that they can feel bold and have a good time. But there is something that works much better, and that is prayer. Pray for the power to relax and enjoy the dance. For those of you who are socially insecure, these prayers make it so that you have an appropriate form of self-confidence and a fun-loving spirit. Putting your hand into the hand of God can give you social confidence.

Before you leave home to play a basketball game, you can pray about it. You can pray about it again in the

locker room as you are lacing your shoes. Just before the
basketball game is to begin, you can silently and with your
eyes wide open offer a prayer that you will be able to do
your best. Such prayer habits help you to have the
confidence which an athlete needs, and with such confidence and with the Lord's help your abilities are magnified.

The prayer the Lord always answers is the prayer
wherein we ask him to help us overcome discouragement.
If we will cooperate by "trying" he will always help us
get started again. Sometimes the answer he gives is only a
prompting to "stand up." But once you have stood up and
started to move toward your destiny, the problem seems to
dissolve.

You can of course talk to the Lord without moving
your lips. You can sit in a classroom and think a prayer, or
walk across campus and in your mind talk to the Lord.
You can pray silently while in the midst of a crowd. But
from time to time, in the quiet of your own room, kneel
down and speak out loud to the Lord. Talk to him as long
as you would like to and say things that you feel in the
depths of your heart. Tell him of your frustrations, your
desires to grow, your desires to be able to meet your
dreams. Ask him to reveal to you what you need to do to
find your destiny.

As you pray he'll show you your weaknesses, for he
has said:

"And if men come unto me I will show unto them
their weakness. I give unto men weakness that they
may be humble, and my grace is sufficient for all men that
humble themselves before me; for if they humble themselves before me, and have faith in me, then will I make

weak things become strong unto them.'' (Ether 12:27.)

As he sees you on your knees calling on him in mighty prayer, he will strengthen you in your weaknesses. The things about which you feel inferior will indeed become your strengths.

Of all prayers that are uttered, there are none more beautiful than the prayer of gratitude—prayers in which we express to the Lord our sincere thankfulness for his goodness to us.

I recall once that while my wife and two young sons and I were at a football game it started to rain. There was a strong wind and the rain was coming in from the north. I knew that there was a strong possibility that the children might want to go home. I didn't want to go home because our team was winning, which wasn't too common in those days. I stretched the little blanket around us as best I could and took one of the boys up on my lap. I put the other one between myself and my wife, who was on the side opposite the way the rain was coming.

I knew that the boy who was sitting on my lap, the youngest one, would be the one that might start to complain, so I paid particular attention to him. I took my handkerchief out and tried to wipe the rain from his head. Periodically I then wrung out the water from the totally drenched handkerchief and wiped him again. I really tried to protect him from the rain. I also told him things such as, ''The man is going to kick the ball, and the other man is going to try to catch it.'' Through it all my young son maintained a cheerful disposition.

The game progressed until finally it was almost over, and although we were drenched our team had secured the victory. About that time the sun broke through the clouds.

The storm was over. I felt my young son flex his muscles and squirm. I knew that he wanted to leave my lap. He got down and stood on a row of bleachers just below the one I was sitting on. In that position he was able to look straight into my eyes. He stared at me for a few seconds and then he spoke. "Dad, you have done so much for me. Isn't there something I can do for you?" As he said these words my heart swelled up within me. He had touched my soul, and I replied with all the power of my spirit, "Just be my son, just be my son." Then I embraced him.

In life there are some hard knocks to take, but through it all we receive marvelous blessings from the Lord. For such generous and kind treatment it seems appropriate to kneel down and say: "Heavenly Father, you do so much for me. Isn't there something I can do for you?" And then that quiet feeling comes to us, that special feeling wherein he speaks to us and says, "Just be my son, just be my son." And then it almost seems that he takes us in his arms and holds us close. That is religion.

During the days of World War II when it appeared that Great Britain could be defeated, King George VI repeated this quotation to the British people: "I said to the man who stood at the gate of the year, 'Give me a light that I might tread safely into the unknown.' And he said to me, 'Go out into the darkness and put your hand into the hand of God, for that is better than a light and safer than a known way.' "

The Lord tells us in the Doctrine and Covenants: "Be thou humble; and the Lord thy God shall lead thee by the hand, and give thee answer to thy prayers." (D&C 112:10.) I can think of no greater key to feeling special than being truly religious, to have a dream of being like Christ. Keep your language pure, keep the Word of

Wisdom, pay your tithing, offer your prayers, go to church, fulfill your Church duties, read the scriptures, take seminary, and be clean in thought and deed. As you do these things you'll have that special spiritual feeling in your heart. It will help you to overcome a multitude of problems. You'll live your life based upon the foundation of Christ, and as you do that you cannot fall. You'll be special forever.

Chapter 8
Looking Special

As my wife and I entered a motel in a small town in Kentucky, the lady working at the desk watched us very closely. After we had signed the registration, she asked, "Who are you?" I replied, "My name is George Durrant, and this is my wife Marilyn."

"I don't mean your names," the lady explained. "I mean, who are you?"

I responded, "We are missionaries of The Church of Jesus Christ of Latter-day Saints."

"I knew you were something special," she said with enthusiasm. "I could tell by the way you look."

I was in a good mood, and I jokingly responded, "You mean that I look handsome?"

"Oh no, no, you aren't handsome," she quickly replied. "As a matter of fact, you're not good-looking. It's just that you look good."

Since then I have often thought about the fact that you don't have to be good-looking to look good. That's a great thing to know. That's the real secret of being truly beautiful.

We can't change our facial profile or our physical height, but we can change our countenance, the way we look. The word *countenance* is the term used to describe the sum total of all our facial features and even our body posture. But it's more than that. It's a combination of eyes, nose, lips, expression, added to a special something that comes from within. All this together gives a person his countenance. And the part which comes from within is the most important of all the factors in determining the way we look. It's that which is in the heart that in the long run really determines beauty.

Through one of his prophets, Christ spoke of countenance. He tells us in the Book of Mormon, " ... look up, having the image of God engraven upon your countenances." (Alma 5:19.) As you come to have his image in your countenance, people will look into your eyes and see something special there. And as they do they will love you.

My son, who was then fourteen, once really unlocked his heart and told me some of his deepest concerns. Among other things he said, "Dad, I just don't like the way I look."

I replied, "I don't understand that. You look just like me."

He smiled and sort of ignored my comment as he said, "I just wish I was taller and huskier. I wish I looked more like an athlete."

We often worry about our physical stature and about our "looks." But wishing will not make us suddenly taller. Jesus asked, "Which of you by taking thought can add one cubit unto his stature?" (Matthew 6:27.)

My son wanted to be taller, but all the food he could eat and all the things he could do didn't seem to make him

68

taller. Others want to quit growing; they think they're too tall already, yet they grow on and on. Some wish they were huskier. Others wish their figure were more trim and beautiful. We know that in a limited way and over a period of time there are certain things we can do in regard to our stature, but basically our body size and our facial features are out of our control. It's a common thing to feel that you are not exactly the most handsome or beautiful person in the town. Most of us would really like to be beautiful or handsome, and when we feel we are not it creates a problem for us.

It might seem difficult to believe, but these physical things are of secondary importance to our "good looks." I know that you might disagree, but I ask you to believe me at least a little bit. The thing that really matters and that supersedes all else in determining how we appear is how we feel in our heart. The best way to describe these feelings of the heart is with the word *attitude*.

A girl came to my office and wanted to talk to me. After talking about some rather unimportant matters, she became very serious. She said, "I have something else I want to talk about."

"What's that?" I inquired.

"I don't want to be this tall," she said. "I'm taller than many of the boys. I haven't been getting any dates. I think one reason is that there are only a few boys taller than me and that limits me so much." She went on to say, "I wish I hadn't grown so tall."

"That's interesting," I said, "because ever since I first saw you in my class I've admired your tallness. That is what makes you look like a model."

69

"Yes, but how do you get to be a model?"

I replied, "I don't know, I've never been a model. But to me you sure look like one. I like the way you stand up straight to the full extent of your height."

She seemed to feel a little better, but she added longingly, "I just wish I could get more dates."

"If you keep close to the Lord and as you stand up straight as you do," I said, "you'll get more dates. At least you'll get the important dates with the right guy. Until you do you'll just have to keep doing good—and I know you are good because I see in your countenance something very special."

This beautiful girl is one of the multitude of people who wonder about their physical stature. While I was a bishop another girl came to my office. She too wondered why she felt so insecure and why she had so few friends and wasn't getting any dates at all. I had noticed her for a period of months and had felt that she wasn't keeping herself as neat as she could have. I'm not an expert in how girls should apply makeup or how they should comb their hair, but I could tell that her eyebrows and other parts of her face were improperly made up.

As we talked she expressed to me her feelings that no one cared about her, that only I, her bishop, had any sincere interest in her. She asked me a question. "What can I do, how can I improve?" As I thought about the question I felt impressed to reply, "Before I say what I'm going to say I want you to know that I do love you and that I do care. But there are some things that you need to hear."

I went on, "I don't think you're taking care of yourself properly. I don't think your hair is as lustrous and

70

well kept as it might be. I feel that your makeup is being improperly applied. I feel that your dresses could be more lovely." She started to cry. I said, "Go ahead and cry, but you need to hear these things."

She continued to cry as I added, "I'm not going to leave this matter by telling you what is wrong. I'm going to ask a girl in our ward who knows about beauty and charm to be your counselor. And I want you to go to her and follow her advice."

Amidst her tears she said, "I won't do it."

"Now, as your bishop, I call you to do that," I said firmly. After many more tears she agreed. I called the other girl in and the two of them got together. A few days later I moved from the town to another assignment.

It was about a year later that I returned to my former place of employment. As I was walking down the sidewalk on the campus a girl came toward me. I didn't notice her much at first, but it soon became obvious that she was on a collision course with me and she wasn't about to turn aside. I stopped and she reached out her hand and said, "Bishop, I'm so glad to see you!"

I was confused as to who she was and said, "Now let's see, do I know you?"

She said, "Bishop, don't you know who I am?" With a most warm smile she said her name. Then I remembered our experience together and I could see that it was the girl I had assigned to improve her appearance. The only words I could think of to say were "You're beautiful!"

"And furthermore," she said, "I'm going to get married."

She had combed her hair in a way that was becoming

to her, her makeup was just right for her face, and her dress was a color that somehow complemented her complexion. She had started to care about her appearance and was doing all she could to make herself beautiful. In so doing she had developed an inward pride and in her heart she had a more special feeling. I could tell by a difference not only in her overall grooming but also in her countenance. She seemed to glow, and as I walked away I knew I had just had the joy of seeing a truly beautiful person.

It has been my observation that many girls, particularly in high school, never quite arrive at their full beauty. That is, their poise and thus their beauty comes slowly. On the other hand, some girls while very young are cute and pretty and they really capture the high school boys. Such girls are popular and they are the toast of the school. There are certain other girls who, although they are not the most physically attractive, have the kind of personality that makes them very much the leaders and among the most popular in the school. But there are some, quite a few, who while in high school are sort of "wallflowers." They're not in the mainstream of high school popularity. Some girls are close to being in the limelight but they aren't quite there, and the range goes from there all the way to some who hardly seem to have any friends at all. Often a high school girl feels that if she isn't among the most popular, life is almost unbearable. Sometimes, in an effort to gain recognition, a young woman is tempted to go out and act improperly with boys just for the sake of having someone pay attention to her; or she might retreat into a social shell and thus add to her insecure feelings.

Many problems could be avoided if you would be patient and realize that the high school days are not the end but really just the beginning. You should be advised also

72

that high school boys don't always recognize true beauty. If they don't notice you it's probably because of their lack of appreciation for beauty rather than your lack of beauty.

After high school many girls gain a kind of poise and awareness and charm that makes them among the most beautiful of all women. And boys, as they become mature, see with different eyes. Often at school reunions many of the most attractive girls present are not those who were the toast of the high school.

With these things in mind I offer a special message to you girls who don't date a lot in high school and don't consider yourselves to be the belle of the ball. If you will continue to take the best physical care of yourself you possibly can, if you learn to sew so that you can have proper clothing, if you learn to comb your hair in the way that seems just right for your face, if you learn to apply makeup with modesty and skill, if you love people, and most importantly if you keep the commandments of the Lord and particularly the commandment concerning virtue, you will pile up "scones" in your heart; and as you do so you will become truly beautiful. Then you'll know that it has been worth it, because something special will happen to you.

The Book of Mormon describes the destruction which preceded the coming of the resurrected Christ to the American continent. After the terrible three days of darkness, he came. He talked to the people, healed their sick, blessed their children and administered the sacrament to them. Finally he told them to go to their homes and promised to come again the next day. Undoubtedly these people excitedly told those who had not been present at his first visit that Christ had come and would come again the next day.

Try to imagine in your mind that you are preparing for the next day and for the journey that will take you to where Christ will appear. You are trying to determine how to dress. How will you try to look so that when he sees you he will see you as you really are? Modesty would suggest that the thing you would want him to look upon would be your countenance, and particularly your eyes. You would want to dress so that he would notice that you seemed to be well groomed and appropriately dressed, and that your eyes sort of sparkled and shone.

This doesn't mean that every day you need to dress in your Sunday best, but you should always dress modestly so that people will first notice your eyes. Let your eyes and your countenance speak for you. If your eyes or your countenance are to speak well for you, you must have purity in your heart. Remember the words of Alma: "I say unto you, can ye look up to God at that day with a pure heart and clean hands? I say unto you, can you look up, having the image of God engraven upon your countenances?" (Alma 5:19.)

If you are to have the image of God engraven upon your countenance, you must have clean hands and a pure heart. If you are to be beautiful, you must be clean. You must not allow immodest behavior to have any part in your life. If you do, it will darken the light of Christ within you, and when people look into your eyes they will see that the image of God is not in your countenance.

Yes, it's possible to look good without being good-looking. And when you look good, special people are attracted to you. And when they look at your countenance they will feel that you are beautiful or handsome. For those of you who don't date much, both young men and young women, if you continue to "look good" because

74

you are good, someday when the time is right someone will come along who looks with the right kind of eyes. Then you'll have found a special someone who will be attracted to you because he will see in you someone special. And he or she will say of you, "You are the most beautiful person in all the world."

Chapter 9
Goofing Off in a Special Way

I recall a time when I had an appointment to see a very important man. As I entered his office I was a bit nervous. His first question to me was "How are you?" I replied, "Nearly perfect!" He seemed pleasantly startled and asked, "Oh, is that right? Just what is it that is keeping you from being completely perfect?" I quickly replied, "I lie a little." I thought for a minute he might fall out of his chair with laughter. The atmosphere in the office was no longer stressful for me, because he and I had had a laugh together. There's something about laughing together over wholesome things that binds people's hearts together.

For that reason, on the list of admirable personality qualities I list "goofing off good" very highly. By "goofing off good" I mean that I like people who know how to laugh and have fun in an appropriate way. When things get a little stressful, they can say or do something that brings some humor to the situation. A good kind of humor is most soothing at the right time.

I remember once walking to junior high school. As I walked down the Old Mill Lane, I was dreaming about a certain girl. I wondered how I could impress her, how I could make her think I was special. As I was walking along, just before I got to the school, I saw an Oldsmobile car pass by. My creative mind quickly fashioned a joke about the name "Oldsmobile." I decided that I would tell my joke to the special girl. I would say to her, "Have you ever seen a smobile?" And she would reply, "No, George, I haven't. I don't even know what a smobile is. What is it?" And I would say, "A smobile is a car. I saw a smobile this morning. But it was an old one. It was an old smobile." By the time I walked the last few yards to school I had that speech well rehearsed.

(I'm glad I got to record this most excellent little joke in this book. It gives me an opportunity to show you that along with the problems I had as a young fellow, I also had some strengths. For you can see from this fine joke that I was very clever. Perhaps this joke is not as clever in the 1970s as it was in the 1940s, but back in those days it was really quite a joke.)

Clever as the joke was, it didn't help my relationship with the girl because that day, when I saw her, she made me so nervous that I couldn't remember all my lines. Therefore I didn't tell her this most humorous story. And as a result, another day passed without her thinking of me as being special.

Sometimes it is hard for you, as it was for me, to be able to "goof off good." There is something within us that holds us back. Until we gain our self-confidence, we have a hard time "goofing off good." The immature and the insecure know that humor is one key to popularity. Therefore they "goof off," but they do so in a *bad* rather than a good way. Such people make fun of others and make light of sacred things. There are those who in attempts to be funny are willing to belittle both themselves and others. They are not able to discern that there are times to be funny and times to be serious. In an attempt to win attention they destroy property. They make loud inappropriate "cat calls" during programs and movies. They destroy school and church classes by giving light-minded answers during discussions.

If you desire to be special, you must avoid such inappropriate humor as though it were poison. For indeed it is. It kills almost all the good that makes one a special person. Thus we see that humor, like almost all things, has two sides. One side is godly and the other is satanic.

The right kind of humor is difficult to incorporate into our lives. Therefore you have to work at it. It's a blessing to be born with a sense of humor, but if you weren't born with such a virtue it's possible to develop it. Like all talents, it must be developed through practice, through prayer, and through good taste.

"Goofing off good" helps us to avoid the trap of taking all things a bit too seriously. I recall a fellow in a seminary class I once taught. I noticed that during the devotional (the first part of the class wherein we sang, prayed, and read scriptural passages), he would always close his eyes. He wouldn't open his eyes until we had completed this part of the class period. Whenever this fellow would come to see me, he never talked about anything except the most serious of subjects. One day I asked him, "Why do you close your eyes during the devotional?" He replied: "Brother Durrant, I just don't want to see any of those other guys in the class during the time we are worshipping the Lord." "Why is that?" I asked, and he replied, "They are filthy, no-good people."

A bit surprised, I asked, "Is that so?" He quickly responded. "When those guys dress in the locker room over at the gym, they use foul-mouthed language and they take the Lord's name in vain. Listening to them turns me sick, and because of that, when we have devotional, I'm not going to open my eyes and look at those kind of people.''

I understood his point. I agree that to be foul-mouthed is to be low indeed. But I wondered if closing his eyes during devotional was really going to help anything. Those fellows had some good qualities about them too. My friend wasn't going to help them get over their bad qualities by closing his eyes during devotional.

By closing his eyes he seemed to be closing inside his heart a sort of hatred for the other young men. He was bottling up inside himself feelings that were making him a miserable and lonely man.

But what could he do? His hatred of filthy language was as it should be. But his method of dealing with it was not helping himself nor others. We need to stay in the battle, and appropriate and wholesome humor is a good way to counteract bad language and dirty jokes. If we can be the master of many ''corny'' stories we can use these as a counterattack on filth. When we hear a dirty joke we can ignore it and tell a corny joke. By so doing, one person can change the course of the conversation of an entire group. Getting people to laugh about good things can divert them from laughing about filthy things.

While in the army barracks, I heard many filthy things. Such talk disgusted me. But I didn't feel I could allow others to make me disgusted all the time. I don't really enjoy being disgusted. I find that being disgusted all of the time is disgusting. I had to live in the barracks, unless I wanted to sleep outside. So I'd counterattack their filth with my corny humor. I'd say such things as: ''I was raised on a farm where we had chickens and we sold eggs for a living. I used to have to work around those chickens, and that is where I first learned to dislike "foul" language." About the chickens, I added, "I didn't like their *yokes* at all. It seemed that they were always *egging* me on." And to get even more corny, I'd say: "I had a pig on that farm. We called him *Ball Point*. That wasn't his real name but it was his *pen name*. He got lonely and we couldn't afford another pig, so I drew a big picture of a pig and put it in his pen. It wasn't a real pig, but it was a good *paper mate*." I could go on and tell you more of what I told those guys, but I'll spare you the rest. Anyway, such stories seemed to overpower their vulgarity—at least in part. I'd kid them along, and in so doing I could talk them into cleaning things up a little. Gradually things changed. I came to have a deep love for those men and I believe they felt the same toward me. But it was humor and not disgust that provided the oil to make things run more smoothly.

I like the kind of jokes that Jack Benny told. He told jokes about being stingy with his money when in reality he was most generous. He also kidded in his later years about being thirty-nine years old. Nobody got hurt by those kind of jokes, yet he made the whole world laugh and feel better.

As for myself, I often kid about being handsome. I say, "Going on a mission makes a man more handsome, and I've been on two!" People can look at me and know that I'm just kidding (even though I'm not, because I really am handsome). But when I talk that way it seems to break down barriers between people. I notice that as we laugh together it makes us more capable of being serious together. And through this wide range of emotions there is a better chance that we will understand each other and love

80

each other. Thus we will be able to deal with matters that might not be easily dealt with unless we did a little laughing in between our serious business.

I visited often with the fellow who closed his eyes during devotionals. I tried to use an overdose of humor on him and gradually I was able to get him to laugh. Then one day I noticed that he opened his eyes during devotional. I don't know that the guys had repented in the locker room, but I think the chances were greater now that he would have something to do with their repentance. We can't compromise our principles to the least degree, but we can learn to laugh more. When we do, we seem to be able to learn to love more.

One time, while I was teaching seminary, we really sang well. There was a particularly good spirit in the classroom and the song was keyed in such a way that the guys could reach the high notes. We sang with great gusto, and I was so impressed that I was looking up at the ceiling, enjoying myself in singing. It came time for the second verse, and I boomed out with the first few words. To my surprise and embarrassment, I found myself singing a solo.

I looked around the classroom and noticed that Robert, the young man who had been playing the piano, was no longer at the piano bench. He had returned to his seat on the front row. I looked down to where he sat and said, "Robert, we want to sing more of that song." With a broad grin he replied, "I'm sorry, Brother Durrant, but I only know how to play the first verse." I arose from my chair and went over to where Robert was. I struck him playfully on the arm, and then as I looked down at him I burst into great laughter. Oh, how I loved Robert! How could you help but love someone who could make such an announcement!

I feel that the Lord understood that moment and that perhaps he too was gently laughing at Robert. I believe that good humor is the kind wherein we feel that the Lord would laugh and humor in bad taste is the type that would make him want to cry. Robert was one of those who often "goofed off good." I wouldn't really know what to expect when I'd walk into the classroom each day. But when it came time to be serious, Robert's eyes would open wide and he would listen with all the intensity he could muster. Often, when we talked of the Savior and of the spiritual things of life, I could even perceive that there were tears in his eyes. Then, when we got through with the serious business, once again there would be some humor coming from Robert. He made the seminary class a joyous thing to be part of. Robert had the rare and almost perfect gift of knowing how to "goof off good." His humor was always kind. His words and deeds never hurt anyone's feelings. He never made light of sacred things.

Later Robert went on a mission. Shortly after he had returned home I had the good fortune of meeting his mission president. He asked me if I knew Robert and I said I did. The president said, "Robert, with his humorous ways, caused us all to love him so much that we all cried when he ended his mission." The president continued: "Because of his ability to make people laugh and then turn around and make them cry, he was one of the most influential missionaries we had during my entire mission."

Yes, it's a great gift to be able to make people laugh about good things. But it's a great curse when you rely on speaking inappropriately or making fun of people in an attempt to gain a laugh. That's Satan's form of humor, not the Lord's.

One who has the ability to "goof off good" has a choice relationship with his teachers in school and in church. Such a person senses that when a class becomes rowdy, he or she should not join in that rowdiness. Many times, in our church classes, people sit and nudge one another and laugh at sacred things and do not cooperate with the teacher; and the teacher's heart is broken, as is his spirit. We should never goof off in such a way that a teacher or anyone else gets hurt. Never become a part of a situation that causes a teacher to want to give up teaching.

"Goofing off good" requires great maturity. It's possible to make ourselves and other people laugh and at the same time to always be respectful of the feelings of others. "Goofing off good" requires great talent, because it's an art. As you strive to master this art, and as it becomes part of your personality, people will laugh with you and they will love you. And they will say in all sincerity, "You are really special."

Chapter 10
Out of High School as a Free Agent

One of the Lord's blessings to us is the help that he gives us so that we can graduate from high school as a free agent. By that I mean the help he gives us while we are young which allows us to get out of high school without having any binding agreement with any one particular person of the opposite sex.

Where I taught school, some of the seniors left right after graduation and drove to a nearby state to get married. Such marriages have some chance of being filled with happiness and success, but it seems to me that those involved in such early matrimony would have been more fortunate if they could have had some years after high school before they were married.

It will be a great blessing for you if you make it through high school without feeling that you have found the "right one." Such a major blessing is often made up of the minor blessing of not getting to date very often in school. For those of you who are not so blessed—that is, those of you who do date a great deal in high school—it is an advantage to you if you date a great many different people instead of just one.

During my high school days the Lord blessed me with a very timid nature. At that time, this lack of boldness did not seem like a blessing to me. But now as I look back I know that my shyness in large measure kept me free. I was not what one would describe as "outgoing" in high school. I longed to be the most glamorous and bold fellow in the school, but my timidity kept me from following such a foolish dream.

As I related in chapter 3, as a sophomore I once saw an older student going down the hall with his arm around a girl, and I thought to myself, "That's what I'm going to do when I get to be a junior in high school." When I became a junior, I saw a senior walking down the hall with his arm around a girl, and I thought, "When I get to be a senior I'm going to walk down the hall with my arm around a girl and be a big wheel." But when I was a senior I was still timid. So I decided that I would wait until I got in college before I would walk down the hall with my arm around a girl. Then in college I decided I'd wait until after my mission.

There were two reasons why in high school I didn't walk down the hall with my arm around a girl. One was the characteristic I've already related, namely, my timidity. The other reason was that there wasn't any big rush on the part of any girl to walk down the hall with my arm around her. But now I look upon these formerly painful circumstances as a blessing to me, because that made it easy for me to graduate from high school free from any commitment to any girl.

I wasn't quite dateless in high school. I went out on dates as many as three or four times. I recall my first date. It was between my sophomore and junior year. There was a girl who I thought was most special above all other girls. I didn't dare talk to her face to face, because being in her presence made me nervous.

Someone Special—Starring Youth

It was summer. I lived some distance from her in another part of town, but one of my school mates was her paperboy. One day I asked him if he ever saw her as he delivered his paper, and he said he did. He reported that she was sometimes out mowing her lawn or working in the yard. Feeling bold because she was at least a mile away, I said, "If you see her again would you ask her if she would go to the movie with me a week from Friday?" He said he would. I had almost forgotten the matter when about a week later he delivered our paper and said, "Hey, I saw her today and I asked her if she would go to the movie with you and she said she would." I was amazed that she had accepted.

I remember thinking that if I had known she would accept I wouldn't have asked. A bad case of nervousness set in. My daydreams told me that I was happy about the upcoming date but the reality of it all frightened me almost beyond my emotional limits.

A friend who had access to his father's car promised me that he would get a date so that we could go together, but his efforts failed and I had to go *alone*. I had just received my driver's license but the only vehicle our family owned was a pickup truck. It was hard to shift into second gear in this vehicle without grinding the gears. I thought, "If I take her out and try to shift it into second and grind the gears she'll think I'm dumb." So I decided to walk on the date.

The night finally arrived. Almost in panic, I walked the several blocks to her house. I knocked on the door and there she was. We walked down to the local theater. As we passed the candy and popcorn counter, I had to use all my nerve to ask her if she would like something. She said, "Why don't you just get some popcorn." So I did—one box. As we were watching the movie I would wonder to myself, "Should I offer her some popcorn now?" Then I would think, "What if she says no when I offer her the popcorn? What would I do then? I couldn't stand to be rejected." I'd tell you what the movie was about but I couldn't seem to concentrate on that. The only scene I recall was the one that said "The End."

We walked home from the movie at a fast but silent pace. I recall the feeling of joy I had as her door closed and she was on the other side and I was on my way home. I felt as if I had just been freed from the most restrictive situation I had been in, and I was so grateful that it was over. But in the next few blocks I was dreaming again of the next time I would take her out. I was sort of a resilient fellow but I sure was timid. I just didn't have the confidence I needed to be a great dater.

I had the blessing of being thus protected from the many pitfalls of early dating. Those of you who aren't so protected, those who could have many dates, you'll just have to protect yourself. Timidity did it for me. You'll have to use good sense and pray to the Lord for help.

As you girls evaluate your dating or lack of it, some of you probably wish that you could go steady. I say to you who wish for such a thing but who get no such results (and I hope you will understand) that perhaps the Lord is taking care of you and that's why you don't get to go out regularly. Later your dating will come. And at that time you will be more ready for it and you will handle it better. Too much dating when you are young can be a dangerous thing in many ways. Many people make moral mistakes on those dates, and others become committed to someone else at too young an age.

The Lord made some of us timid, or at least he

supports us in our timidity toward the opposite sex. But someday when we are out of high school and the boy or girl is right, he will help us to be romantically bold. The great experiences of serving as a missionary will make you bold in many ways. Such boldness is timed perfectly—for right after one's mission is the time to be romantically bold.

I recall a classmate of mine who was the opposite of me when it came to his relationship with the girls. He had many dates during high school and was among the most popular boys. He had dark hair and dark eyes, a perfect profile, much charm, and was extremely bold. After high school he went to work as a truck driver and I enrolled in college. I commuted from home to college each day with an older fellow who had a car. One day, right after I had begun college, as we were driving home we passed by my bold classmate's residence. There in his driveway was a new red Chevrolet convertible car. I thought it was the most beautiful car I had ever seen. Later that day I saw him riding around in that red convertible with a beautiful blonde girl. She looked good in that car. I thought that the only thing that could have made that picture more beautiful was for me to have been the owner of that car and the boyfriend of that girl.

A few weeks later there came an invitation to the wedding reception of my handsome friend and the beautiful girl. The wedding ceremony took place in a garden and was performed by a bishop. Three of my friends and I attended the reception together. We had purchased a gift—it was a lamp that was so big that it couldn't be wrapped. We entered carrying the lamp. We gave it to the youngsters at the door and they carried it over to the gift table. I felt glad that we were able to give such a gift.

88

I made my way through the reception line. I was not accustomed to such social situations and I hardly knew what to say to bride or groom. But after awkwardly offering congratulations I took my seat at a table and began to eat my nuts and drink my punch. As I ate I looked across the room to where this handsome couple were being congratulated by well-wishers. I remember thinking: "Why don't I do what they are doing? Why don't I grow up? Why don't I quit school and get myself a car and a girl and get myself married? They're moving forward in life and I'm just going to school. *When will I ever catch up to them?*"

Time went by and I continued to go to college. Then came that glorious day when my bishop asked me if I would like to go on a mission. I replied, "Bishop, I'd give my right arm to go on a mission." So I went. Two years later I came home. By this time my friend had been married for some time and he and his wife were blessed with three children.

Not long after my arrival home from my mission, I was finally bold enough to walk down the hall with my arm around a girl, and I was bold enough, even without the help of a red convertible car, to win the love of a most beautiful girl. She and I went to the temple and there we were married. As the years passed we were blessed to have eight children.

Twenty years after our high school graduation I saw my friend and talked to him. He was still driving trucks for a living. Now, there's nothing wrong with driving a truck; it's an honorable way to make a living. But my friend now told me that he didn't want to drive a truck. He wanted to go to college and learn to be an engineer. Longingly he said: "If only I had gone to school when I was younger! But all that seemed important then was money, cars, and marriage." He confessed: "It's hard to go to college now. I can only go at night, and it's going to take me years and years."

I think perhaps he's still going to college. After our talk, I had time to think. I remembered the question I'd asked myself at his reception so many years ago. "When will I ever catch up with him? And as I thought about these things I had a quiet feeling within my heart that I had indeed caught up. I had also had some other glorious experiences which he hadn't had. I had had the privilege of going to college and the all-important blessing of going on a mission. He had had neither of these experiences.

Now, I'm not measuring myself against him, because he is a choice person and in many ways has talents which far surpass mine. All I'm really trying to say is that it's a blessing to graduate from high school without being involved seriously with those of the opposite sex. It's appropriate to be friendly with them and to go to school dances and such, but how much better it is to save the search for that special one until a little later in life! By doing that you can do some important things between high school and marriage. And then when the time is right, in the natural course of things you can win the love of someone special.

It seems that some people desire to get married while they are very young so that they can use marriage as a means of escaping from home. To you who sometimes want to get away from your parents before high school graduation, I make a special appeal. Stay at home and try to make things better there. If you do, the Lord will bless you. Time goes by quickly. First graduate from high school and then go out and do some things that can only be done then. Have a look around before commiting yourself to marriage. I know the young men and young women in your home town are fine, but what a blessing it is to go to college or a trade school! There you can meet people from other towns and other states. Furthermore, right after high school is the time that you really bloom as a person. During those days there comes into your life a series of circumstances which give you confidence, poise, and social maturity. Some of the prettiest girls at high school reunions are those who make it through high school without being married. And some of them dated but little there. But after high school they gained a certain kind of radiant confidence. They learned more about how to dress and how to comb their hair. They gained the poise that comes from going to school and learning how to do special things. In the days after high school we all become more beautiful or handsome, and we become candidates for romance and marriage with other special people.

In high school we would all like to be popular. Most of us would like to have others look upon us as being able to win the love of the most choice and most popular person in school. But that's not the way it is for many of us. The Lord loves those of us who are in a sense "wall-flowers" and he blesses us with the gift of graduating from high school as a free agent. He also loves those of you who are popular and self-confident. He will bless you if you will remain humble and prayerful. He will give you strength and wisdom so that you also can have some years after high school before you get married.

Be patient, my young friends. If you do, your dreams will come true. While you're waiting you can do those things that put special "scones" in your hearts. Finally

91

your personality will be so attractive that it will manifest itself in your countenance. Someday, to someone, your coming into a room will change everything. Not because you will look like a Greek goddess, but merely because you will look good and because you will be special.

Chapter 11
A Special Vocation or Profession

In my final years of high school I was not at all certain that I wanted to attend college. Toward the middle of my senior year, the vice principal of the school called me into his office and asked me where I was going to go to college. His question took me by surprise and I asked, "Do you think I should go?" He replied, "Sure you should go." A bit humbled, I replied, "I haven't been getting good grades." "That's because you haven't tried," he answered. He continued, "You ought to go to college." "Do you think I could succeed in college?" I asked. His words pierced my heart as he said, "I know you could." As I left his office, I loved him because of what he had said and the way he had said it.

Shortly thereafter a representative of Woodbury College in California was scheduled to come to our high school. Two of my friends and I in a joking manner went around school saying that we were going to Woodbury College. Finally the man came and I talked to him about the college he represented. He really enthused me. For a time I was seriously set upon going to college there. I never did go to that institution because of finances, but I still love Woodbury College because it was part of my earliest dream of going to college. That dream of college came nearer to reality when I decided to go to Brigham Young

University. I was living near there, and in those days it wasn't as difficult to get into college as it is today. Thus I was able to enroll in college.

As I made my way through those early collegiate days I wondered just what I should study in preparation for my life's work. Many of the young men I knew were going into teaching, engineering, accounting, and so on. But I didn't know what to do. I had worked for a while at Geneva Steel, where I became acquainted with a chemist who seemed to have a pleasant job. I thought that I might enjoy being a chemist so I decided to major in chemistry. After half a semester, I was about to sink in a super-saturated solution of things I couldn't understand, and I decided that chemistry wasn't for me. I thus knew that there was one thing I wouldn't be and that was a chemist. So I was a little closer to selecting a major.

But what *would* I be? I went for an entire year to college not knowing what I wanted. I had brothers who were elementary school teachers and I explored the possibility of becoming a teacher. I liked that idea very much. I think I would have enjoyed a career as an elementary school teacher. But I still couldn't really decide what to do.

During this time of indecision I was talking to a friend. He asked me, "What are you going to major in?" I said, "I'm thinking about being an elementary school teacher, but I don't know if I want to stay in that." He replied, "If you're not going to stay in that, what are you going to do?" I scratched my ear and said, "I don't know."

"What are you good at?" he asked. I thoughtfully considered his question and replied, "I guess, nothing."

94

"Oh, don't give me that," he said, a bit sternly. "You're good at something. What do you like? What is it you like to do?" He really had me thinking. The only thing I felt good about in my school career was when the teachers asked me to draw or color a picture. That was something I felt that I could do better than most of the other kids.

I told my friend of the time when I was in the sixth grade and was sitting at my desk drawing. At the time my class had a mean teacher; but he was fair, because he was mean to each of us. I remember that as I was working away he came down the aisle and stood by my side. I knew he was there and it made me nervous. He watched what I was doing and finally he reached over and grabbed my paper from me without saying a word. He strode up to the front of the room, he held my work up before the class, and said: "This is what I mean. Do it the way George does it."

I concluded my recital of this incident by saying: "That was one of the highlights of my elementary school career. And as the school years passed by, I always liked art."

My friend then asked, "Did you take any art classes in high school?" I replied, "I didn't take art in high school because none of my friends did." When this fellow had heard all that I had to say, he said, "George, you should major in art." "Can you major in art?" I asked. "I didn't know you could major in some enjoyable thing like that." His reply was: "Sure you can. I'm majoring in drama." So it was decided I would major in art.

The next semester I took an art class. I did my best at painting a watercolor landscape and I felt pretty good about it. Just after I finished this first painting, something happened that I didn't know would be part of art classes. The teacher said, "Let's put all of our paintings up front and invite the class members to criticize each one." I was shocked at this procedure and thought, "I'd sooner sit on my painting than put it up in front for people to criticize." But I had no choice, and soon my picture was there for all to see.

After my classmates had talked about several of the other pictures they came to mine. I had little confidence and my heart pounded with anticipation of the criticism. One girl spoke first and said, "I like the way he did the sky." I was thrilled as I looked at my sky. I thought, "By George, that is a good sky." After a few positive comments, the students suggested some things that were wrong with the painting. But after they had told me there was something right about my work I didn't mind knowing there was something wrong about it. I decided then and there that on my next painting I'd do the right things better and I'd correct the wrong things. After that I looked forward to hanging paintings before the class for their criticism. Gradually I became an artist, and I loved art.

One teacher was particularly good to me. He had the duty of grading all of my oil paintings. He gave me very high grades. One day I got my courage together and I asked him, "Sir, do you give me such good grades on my work because the paintings are good or do you do so because you like me?" He replied with a warm smile, "George, it's because I like you." Then he quickly added: "But it's also because your paintings are good. You've got talent. You could be a great artist if you stick with it." Those words meant a great deal to me, coming from him, because I respected him.

I found out so many things when I found out I could

be an artist. I was satisfied that I couldn't be a chemist, but I could be an artist. There are a multitude of things I probably couldn't be good at, but there was at least one thing that I could be good at—art.

After I started becoming an artist all my grades, which to that point in college hadn't been very good, improved dramatically.

In my early days at college I played basketball when I should have been in history and ping pong when I should have been studying sociology. Almost all of my hometown friends dropped out of college after the first year. Then there were only myself and one other fellow still there. He and I were almost always together, but then he got interested in zoology. He would collect insects and I used to go with him to do so. His interest in such things intensified, while mine did not. While he was chasing insects, I felt that there was something more interesting to chase. So I lost the constant companionship of my last hometown friend.

In my second year of college, and before I'd found my art interest, I received my grades for the previous semester. I didn't dare look at this vital document because I knew it would not be a pleasant experience. I walked across campus to a place where I was all alone. Then I mustered the courage to look at my grades on that small but discouraging piece of paper. But as I looked at my grades, which ranged from average to very poor, a thought came into my mind and heart. I believe the thought was prompted by the Lord. It was this simple yet powerful message, "George, you can do better than that." I folded up the paper and walked toward class. I had hope in my heart, for from then on I would do better than that. My grades improved dramatically. It was about that time that I started to get an interest in art. Now I knew what I wanted to be, and the Lord had told me I could do better.

School became a pleasure. I sat as close to the front of the classroom as I could, I took notes on all lectures, I read all the books and wrote all the reports, I talked to the teachers after class. I became interested in learning, and what a thrill that was!

My purpose in relating my experience is not to try to convince all of you to go to college. There is already too much pressure in today's world for almost all young people to go to college. If you feel sure you have a plan better suited to you than college would be, you ought to forget college and pursue that plan. But you must go somewhere and learn something that makes you able to do something better than almost everyone else. You must become a sort of specialist in something if you are to feel special.

Too many people fall into a job right after high school and become trapped for life by that job. They hear of a job running a crane in a factory. Because this work pays well, and because they have no other plans, they take the job. Forty years later they're still working in the same factory. Sometimes they have advanced and have been trained on the job to the point where they are specialists. But often they long to be doing something else. So don't be in too big a hurry to go to a job that you feel you'll pursue all your life. Get some training first.

To get such training some should go to trade school and some to college. Perhaps you are one who really should go to college. You have intellectual ability which has been demonstrated in high school, or at least you know you could do well in school work if you really tried. You usually know how well you could do in college work.

If you feel that college beckons to you, give it a try. There isn't much to lose and there is everything to gain. And if you really want to go and are willing to work you can arrange the finances.

College is a special place. It can open a thousand doors to your future. Some are doors that you didn't plan for, but they are doors that for you are better than any doors you might otherwise have been able to pass through. College graduates don't always earn more money than non-college graduates. And sometimes they can't get jobs in their chosen field. But I've never met a college student who has pursued a positive course who hasn't grown as a person.

It's my hope that if you have an urge for college you'll go after that urge. You can always decide later to go another direction. But with each year that goes by in your life and the responsibilities they bring, it becomes more and more difficult to go back to college. It's a sad thing to see a person regret during most of his life that he didn't go to college while still in his youth. To some of you who should go to college, I say, as my vice principal said to me, "Sure you can make it."

When entering college it's a blessing to know what you want to major in. But if you don't know, that isn't any reason at all for not proceeding. Neither in high school nor in my early college days did I know what I wanted to be, but I knew I wanted to be something. My mother told me I was special and I knew she was right. And when my principal told me I could be a college student I loved him for that. When Woodbury College came along I got enthused about going there. Then at BYU I discovered that I could do good school work. I discovered that I was an artist.

As a youth, you don't have to know exactly where you're going. You just have to know you're going and then move forward. Doors open up for you and you can walk through those doors. You tarry there for a while, then you see other doors; and you walk through those doors. I believe that if you'll pray and plan and go forward the Lord will lead you to a work in which you can make the greatest contribution. But you have to move forward and you have to learn to be prepared.

For those of you who know that you could do good work in high school if you really try, remember that this is the day to make a good academic record in high school or you won't be able to get into college.

I relate the following to those of you who feel that going to college is not for you. In the heat of July I was driving my car down a burning highway in Southern Utah when the whole engine seemed to explode. My entire family was with me. We were thus stranded many miles from a town, and the heat was almost unbearable. I looked at my engine and knew that there was no hope to repair it there. It would have to be towed into a service station.

I hitched a ride with a passing motorist, and while the family waited I went into town. It was the Fourth of July, and I knew help would be hard to find. As we approached town I said a silent prayer. I had to find someone who could help me. There were several service stations in a row. I felt impressed to go to a certain one of them. There I found a young man who was most sympathetic to my plight. He was the manager. He provided a towing service as part of his operation. He and I drove out on the highway and towed the car in. He had his mechanic get right on it but soon found that they couldn't repair it that day because they had to get parts from another bigger city.

100

A Special Vocation or Profession

During this distressing experience this service station manager was totally kind to us. He and I had a heart-to-heart talk. He said he had attended college for a time. He explained, "I sort of wanted to be a medical doctor, but I wasn't sure." He continued, "Then I had a chance to take this station and I knew that I liked this kind of work. I'm happy here and I'm doing well." I thought to myself, "How good it is for me that he turned away from medicine to do this; for if he hadn't, I don't know what I'd have done on this hot day."

He seemed sincerely interested in our family. As we tarried at his station I noticed how he greeted people and how he treated his employees. He had a combination of mechanical ability, business sense, and great confidence. He told people what was wrong with their car and they believed him. He inspired people as he talked to them.

The next day when I drove away from that service station I knew I'd been with a real man. I was glad he had chosen that kind of work. I predict that as he works at that service station and goes forth in his Church work he will become a highly influential person. And that town will be better off because he's there. He'll also bless the lives of many travelers and will be to them what he was to us—a good Samaritan.

To college or to trade school? It doesn't really matter which direction you want to go. All that matters is that you go. It's like walking toward a mountain. You see no way through. You walk right up and almost put your nose against the cliffs, and then you notice that just off to the side there's an opening. It was an opening you didn't know was there, but by walking close to the mountain you found it. You got through that opening only to find that just ahead the way is blocked again. But as you walk

101

toward the apparently insurmountable cliffs you find that there is a way through.

So be faithful and go forward. Don't be side-tracked by some immediate thing that seems attractive when in reality you know you should go beyond. Pray to the Lord to be guided to what you should do for a living. As you do so, and as you work, you will arrive at your destined occupation.

What a blessing it is when a girl goes to college or a trade school! If she never enters the profession or vocation for which she has trained, that doesn't matter, because every positive thing that she learns makes her a better person and helps her teach her children. It is through having educated and inspired mothers that we are able to raise the kind of children that will make the world a better and happier place. If your dream in high school is to someday get married and be a mother, then you had better get educated to be that. Study cooking, sewing, accounting, business, child psychology, and all the things that make a mother. Move forward toward your dream. If you desire to study to be the best school teacher or nurse there ever has been, and then you don't get to be that, you'll probably end up being among the greatest mothers.

Decide what you want to do for a living on a basis other than the money involved. If your goal in choosing your life's work is merely to become rich, you'll often be thirsty; because riches cannot quench the thirst in the depths of a man's soul. His soul tells him that, although he has wealth, he does not have satisfaction. That is not to say, of course, that there are not professions that are desirable for satisfaction that also result in much wealth.

We should follow those goals that we feel would

102

make a contribution to our fellowmen and bring us inward satisfaction. As a teacher, I feel that there is no life's work in which you can make a greater contribution than that of a teacher.

May the Lord bless you in choosing what you want to do for a living. There's something special for you to do, and if you prepare yourself by making an honest and prayerful effort you will in time find your life's work. Effort, planning and prayer will get you where you need to go. And when you get there you'll feel special. You'll feel like saying: "What I'm doing is the most important thing in the world. I wouldn't trade places with anyone." Others will think, "I'd like to be like him and do what he does because he's special."

Chapter 12
The Priesthood Makes You Special

A bishop once told me of a fellow who had grown up in his ward. This fellow had served a mission, and shortly after his arrival home the bishop was interviewing him. He said, "Bishop, a lot of the girls seem to be interested in me. They look at me as if I'm really something. It wasn't that way before I went on my mission. What's made the difference?" The bishop replied, "Don't you know?" The young man responded: "I think I do. It's the priesthood isn't it, Bishop?" The bishop nodded his head in agreement.

Yes, the priesthood makes men more special, and people are attracted to special people. The world's greatest need is for righteousness. And priesthood men have the opportunity to be the fountainhead of righteousness. But with opportunity comes responsibility, and responsibility can be heavy.

As a deacon, one of the greatest challenges I ever faced was that day when I first passed the sacrament. I wasn't at all sure that I could do it. My fears were somewhat soothed when before the meeting one of the other deacons said, "You go to the front and start there and then you come back this way and I'll start back here and we'll meet right there." He laid out the plan. I knew that all I had to do was follow that plan, but I wondered if it wouldn't have been easier to remain eleven years old instead of turning twelve. Nevertheless it was exciting for me to take the bread and water and distribute it to the people. As we deacons sat back down after the task was completed I felt good in my soul. I was glad I was twelve.

I recall that several months later I was passing the sacrament in a school building where the ward meetings were held while we were building a chapel. I had to go between two rows of chairs that were quite close together. As I did so my Tenderfoot Scout badge got caught in a lady's hair net which was attached to her hat. I couldn't move forward and I didn't know what to do. I finally handed the sacrament tray to someone who was sitting there, took the lapel of my coat in one hand and the net in the other and ripped them apart. The lady seemed startled, but I had broken loose and I proceeded on with passing the sacrament. I didn't want anything to stop me from being successful in my priesthood duty, but I also knew that other snags would come. Priesthood often requires breaking free from obstacles that would hold us back.

Once while I was collecting fast offerings, a task that I didn't really like to start on, an old lady called me into her house. She asked me if I was one of the Durrants. I told her that I was. She gave me the fast offering money and then she got out a big apple pie. She cut me a generous portion. She told me that she thought I was the most handsome of all the Durrant children. I thought, "She sure is a smart woman." She added, "There's just something special about you."

I remember coming out of that house that day having done my priesthood duty. Eating that first piece of pie and the second one made me feel the joy of being a full priesthood brother.

It was a special thrill for me when I became old enough and was ordained a priest, because then I could bless the sacrament. During the sacrament song I'd sing along as we sang those verses which gave us the time to break the bread into small pieces. Then I would have the privilege of kneeling down and saying aloud the sacramental prayer. I tried to say it with all the feeling I could muster.

During those years I found it to be a struggle to always keep the commandments. One of the things that helped me most was the regular opportunity I had to bless the sacrament. I remember many times standing up after saying that prayer, handing the trays to the deacons and looking at the congregation. People looked up at me as if they thought I was special, and I felt special.

That was during the very time I couldn't quite make the basketball team. It was also during the days when I wasn't that popular with the girls. It was at a time when I wanted to be student body president, or even vice president, or even a class representative. It was at a time when I felt really insignificant at school. But at church when I blessed the sacrament I felt special. If I hadn't felt special on those occasions I don't know what would have become of me.

It's marvelous that young fellows like you and me have the privilege of blessing the sacrament. This church is the Lord's church and it gives us opportunities to act for Jesus Christ. And that is special.

Between my freshman and sophomore years at college I was working in a small town. One night I was sitting in a smoke-filled room. It was smoke that I was not helping to create, but I was there. As I sat there I believe I heard the voice of the Lord in my heart. I heard him say to me,

"George, you don't belong here." I got up and left and never went back to that room or any other room like it.

About that time I heard Matthew Cowley, a member of the Quorum of the Twelve Apostles, speak at a devotional assembly at BYU. I didn't know the Church was true at the time, but as he spoke about miracles I received a deep impression that this good man who radiated such love was telling me the truth. I decided that because he told me that the Church is true, it is.

A month later the stake president called me into his office and asked me many questions and explained several gospel principles to me. After I had responded, he said, "We are going to confer upon you the Melchizedek Priesthood and ordain you to the office of an elder." As I left that interview I had a kind of feeling I had never had before. I got in my old car, which seemed to start better now that it knew I was going to be an elder. I drove down to one end of the American Fork business district and made a U-turn and drove down to the other end. As I was driving I was thinking, "This is a great town. I'm glad I live here."

I made another U-turn and drove down to the other end of town where there was a malt shop owned by a man named Don. That's where all the youth of the town went to socialize. Don was smart. He always employed pretty girls. As I walked in there that night I walked taller than I had ever walked. I went up to one of those stools near the counter and sat down. I felt special, and I think I even looked that way, because one of the girls hurried right over and said, "What would you like, George?" I smiled confidently and replied, "I'd like a cherry-chocolate milk shake with more cherry than chocolate." She responded, "I'll fix it just the way you like it."

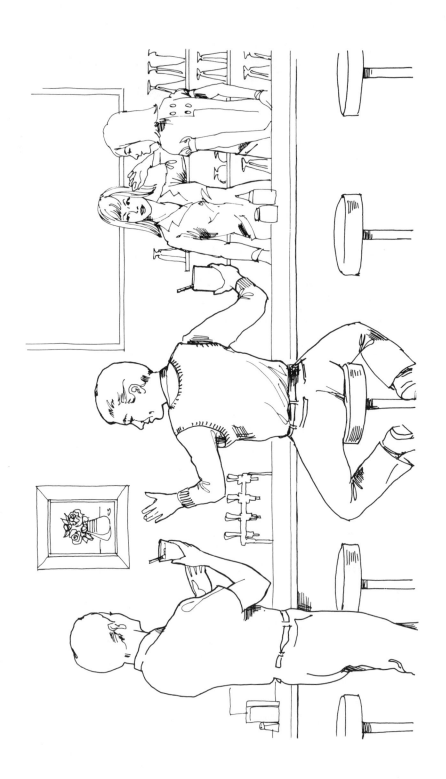

As she started the mixing machine the other girls came over and talked to me. As people would come in I would say a warm "Hi" and smile. I just seemed to want to talk to people and be cheerful because they were all my friends.

I looked at the back wall of Don's shop and there was a painting of some roses. It was a painting that I had painted. I thought, "Those are beautiful roses. I'm a good artist."

As I sat there sipping that delicious milk shake I felt good. I remember that I thought to myself, "I'm a neat guy." I don't mean to sound proud, but as I sat there knowing that I'd soon be an elder I had a feeling that I had something special to offer.

I left Don's after enjoying the last drop of the cherry-chocolate milk shake and drove to my home. I had a bedroom of my own now that the older brother and sisters were married. There in that little bedroom I knelt down and told Heavenly Father that if he'd let me be an elder, I'd really strive to be a good one. I promised him I'd never tell a dirty story or use his name in vain. I'd try to be totally honest and keep myself clean. A peaceful feeling filled my soul as I lay down, and with the joyous thought that I was going to be an elder I drifted off to sleep.

The next week I became Elder George D. Durrant, and I've never gotten over the thrill of that.

Shortly after I became an elder I went home teaching. I was in the company of my former seminary teacher, a teacher who had taught me much and tolerated me a good deal.

We visited an older lady who was so ill that she

couldn't get out of her chair. When she heard our knock she called out for us to come in. She was very grateful for our visit. As we were preparing to leave, she asked us if we could administer to her. It was then I realized that I didn't know how to administer to the sick. I felt relieved when I learned that she had no oil. My companion told her we'd go and get some and be right back. As we drove to his home to get the oil I said apologetically, "I don't know how to give an administration." He understandingly replied, "George, I'll tell you how." Then he taught me what I should say and what I should do in that ordinance of the priesthood.

We came back to the lady's house and I anointed her head with oil. Then I said the words I had been instructed to say. My companion's hands joined mine on her head and he sealed the anointing and gave her a mighty blessing. At the conclusion of the blessing she was able to stand. As she did so she grasped my hand in both of hers and gripped it tightly. Tears streamed down her face as she said with emotion: "George, you are such a special person. I'm glad you are the kind of man that could help give me a blessing." She held my hand for some time as tears came to my eyes.

As I walked out of her home into the cold night air I knew that I had found my "pan of scones." I wanted with all my heart to be the kind of man who could give people blessings. Of course, I knew I couldn't always do it by the laying on of hands. Usually my blessings would need to be in service, or in words of encouragement, or even in a smile. I just wanted to be a blessing to everybody I met. And that kind of feeling made me feel special.

The priesthood does make the difference. It can make a rather ordinary man into a very special man if he is willing to accept the responsibility and serve. Have as one of your major dreams that of being or marrying a priesthood man—someone who is honest, someone who is clean, someone who is true to himself and to his family, someone who serves and thus blesses his fellowmen. With such a dream, with untiring effort and with the Spirit of the Lord, you will become special indeed.

Chapter 13
There Is Life After a Mission

While I was mission president, one of the missionaries who had formerly served in our mission came back to see us. With him he brought his lovely new bride. The two of them visited with us for a few minutes at the mission office. Then, not wishing to take more of our time, they departed.

Soon after their departure, one of the elders who was then serving on the office staff asked if he could have a talk with me. This elder, who was a somewhat deep thinker, came into my office and closed the door. Speaking in most sober tones he said, "President, I just saw the former missionary and his wife." He then leaned forward in his chair and asked, "Does this mean that there is life after a mission?" I smiled and replied with enthusiasm, "Elder, that's exactly what it means."

I repeat that to you, "There really is life after a mission." And life after a mission can be far more glorious than any other kind of life.

As a mission president I have greeted some five hundred missionaries at the airport. A few hours later in each case I've heard the first talk they have delivered in their field of labor. In that first talk given in response to my question, "Why are you here?" many would answer: "I don't know. I just don't know."

Sometimes they would cry, and amidst their tears they would say something such as: "I have a girl friend, and already I miss her so much that I can hardly stand it. I didn't intend to come. At least I didn't intend to come after I found her. But we heard the prophet speak and he said that every young man should go on a mission. I looked at her and she looked at me, and I said, 'Should I go?' and she said, 'Honey, I always wanted to marry someone who has been on a mission.' And I said, 'But we're so much in love.' And she said, 'Yes, we are.' I said, 'Would you wait?' And she said, 'Oh, yes I'll wait.' And I said, 'Should I go?' And she said, 'I think you should.' And I said, 'I think I should too.' "

"And so," he would say, "I'm here. I don't even know the Church is true, and I don't even know if I can do the work. But I'm here, I'm glad I'm here, and I'll really try." Then he'd quit talking and start to cry. And after we had heard him give that first talk, we knew then we had one we could really love.

A month or so later he would stand in a testimony meeting and say something like this: "Elders and Sisters, I didn't know at first why I came, but now I know. The other night we were teaching a family about Joseph Smith. I started to tell that story and something happened to me. I could hardly even speak. The people I was teaching didn't seem to believe me, but suddenly *I* believed me. I found out while I told them of the story of Joseph Smith's first vision that that really did happen. For the first time in my life I truly believed it. I know that story's true. I know that Joseph Smith really did see God and his son Jesus Christ. Now I know why I'm on a mission. I still miss my girlfriend and I miss my parents, but I'd sooner be here than anywhere in the world."

With such a testimony as a foundation he was now

113

free to become a great missionary. With such a conviction he was equipped to find his destiny.

Yes, there is life after a mission. I've seen young men become spiritual giants while they were serving the Lord for two years. I've seen other young men who struggled, who had great difficulty in reaching the goals they had set as missionaries. They had many problems and yet through effort they won many battles. They also came home from two glorious years of missionary service prepared to set out on life's course on a firm foundation. Even those who had not overcome all their basic problems could, if they were blessed to marry the right girl, make a great contribution in the Church and to their fellowmen.

Dream a dream of someday being a missionary. As long as you're dreaming such a dream and as long as you realize that you cannot go on a mission unless you are morally clean, you'll stay morally clean. You'll plan for your mission by being good; and as you do so you'll feel special. Perhaps in your youth you will gain a testimony that settles in and lets you know with every fiber of your being that the Church is true, but if that doesn't happen you should always have an intense desire to know. I've never met a missionary who had that kind of desire who didn't soon know with all his soul that the Church is true.

Prior to my mission I received a call to come to the office of my bishop. He said, "George, how would you like to go on a mission?" I could scarcely speak as I answered, "I'd give my right arm to go on a mission." I hadn't always felt that way. But now I did.

I went to the service station where I worked and announced to the boss that I was going. He replied: "That's great, George. You'll be a good missionary.

114

You've been a good employee. When you get home you probably won't want to work here. But if you do, I'll hire you back because a mission will really help you. A mission is the greatest thing that can happen to a young man." He continued. "I've only got one complaint. When I go to church, people stand up and say that they know the Church is true. Now, there's no way to know that, George. These people can't be telling the truth. No one can know the Church is true. All I want from you is the promise that when you get home you'll not stand up and say that you know the Church is true. George, you're too honest to say that." All I could tell him was that I thought it to be true at that moment and that I wouldn't promise anything.

That's the way I felt when I set sail for England. As the boat lay in Southhampton harbor on the night of my arrival I saw reflected in the waters the lights of England. At that time I didn't have a lot of confidence. I felt as if I would never be able to knock on doors and teach the gospel in such a way that those I taught would want to join the Church. I stood on the ship wondering if it would be possible to swim home. But then I prayed to the Lord and said, "All I ask for now is the courage to get off this ship." He gave me that courage. He gave me courage to meet my mission one day at a time.

Shortly after my arrival in Hull, England, I was blessed to teach a family the fact that God has a body of flesh and bones, that Jesus Christ does also, and that the Holy Ghost is a personage of spirit. As I concluded that scriptural discussion I knew that what I had taught was true. As we left that house I boarded the back seat of a tandem bicycle. We pedaled to our apartment, and as we did my head and heart were swimming with the glories of knowing the true nature of God. A few minutes later I knelt by my bed and prayed to my personal Father. I was so glad I was on a mission.

The next week we taught the family that the true church should have twelve apostles and should be guided by revelation through a prophet. A few days later we read in the scriptures that the true church was taken from the earth and was replaced by a church that was not true. After reading these scriptures, the family identified the church that replaced the true church as their church. They said, "If our church isn't true and the true church is gone, and if the true church should have twelve apostles and a prophet, where is that church?" We replied, "We are here to tell you about that true church and we will do that the next time we meet."

It was that very week that our district leader asked me to give a special talk in our missionary meeting about Joseph Smith and his first vision. In my every spare moment I prepared for that talk. I read and reread the account of the first vision and of the life of Joseph Smith.

Finally the time came and I stood before seven other elders to tell the Joseph Smith story. As I began to speak, I said, "Joseph Smith went to the Sacred Grove, and while he was there, in response to his prayer, God and Jesus Christ appeared to him." Having said that, I could speak no more. The Spirit of the Lord settled in upon me and forced tears from my eyes.

I began to cry, a thing I had not done for years; and never had I cried in this way. I looked down at the floor, not knowing where else to look. After a time I gathered myself together enough to look into the eyes of my seven companions. Each of them was also in tears. The Spirit of

116

the Lord was there. As I spoke, I came to know with all my heart and soul that Joseph Smith was indeed a mighty prophet of God.

I talked about the prophet's persecution and finally his martyrdom. When I finished speaking I was a new man. I knew exactly what I needed to know to really live. I knew then as I do now that God lives and that Jesus Christ is his Son. I knew that Jesus Christ was resurrected and that he appeared to Joseph Smith. I knew that it was right to pay tithing; that the Word of Wisdom was the way to live; that the temple was the place to get married; that the prophet then leading the Church was the voice to follow; and that the scriptures were the guide. I knew everything that I needed to know to truly live.

I believe that that day in England I became a man. After that I became the *greatest average* missionary England ever had.

During my mission the Lord stood by my side and gave me answers to my prayers. And I loved being a missionary. It was still hard at times to knock on doors, but I did it. And the more I did it, the more I found that I could do it.

I found that when I got to England the people there thought I was special. They looked at me as though I was a real somebody. I decided that that's what I'd try to be.

I had a glorious mission. I served under the leadership of what I considered to be the best of all mission presidents. He used to look at me in such a way that he inspired me. I never held any great office in the mission, but I had a quiet feeling that the mission president loved me the most. Of course, if you were to see him and ask him, "Did you love Elder Durrant the most?" he'd say,

117

"Not that I remember." And that's because I suppose he made everybody feel the way that I felt.

He made me feel special.

I came home from England feeling better than I had ever felt before. I was greeted at the train by the girl that I later married and also by my mother. I shook hands with the girl and embraced my mother. For it was my mother who first told me that I was special. In her wonderful way she "spoiled" me with love. She planted in me the seeds of the things that made me special. And after embracing her I was free to shake hands again with the girl who would soon take over in helping me to be special.

I was not overburdened with money in those days, but I had the priesthood and I wanted to be good. I felt that Marilyn, my girlfriend, deserved somebody special, so I asked her to marry me.

The reason I loved her so much was that she was special. Her heart was filled with scones. And when two special people get together, is it any wonder that they want to be married in a special place for eternity?

Yes, there's life after a mission. Some of you girls too will go on missions. For those of you who don't go, encourage him to go.

May the Lord bless us all that if we haven't already, this day we will start to be special. Hold onto the rod and build your life upon the foundation of Christ. This is the place, now is the time. If it is to be it is up to *you*. Fill your heart with scones, spiritual scones that will make you truly desirable. Being good will make you look good. The image of God will be engraved in your countenance and the name of Christ will be written in your heart.

And you will be, now and forever, a very special person.